A JAPANESE MEMOIR OF SUMATRA 1945-1946:
LOVE AND HATRED IN THE LIBERATION WAR

Takao Fusayama

A JAPANESE MEMOIR OF SUMATRA 1945-1946: LOVE AND HATRED IN THE LIBERATION WAR

EQUINOX
PUBLISHING
JAKARTA KUALA LUMPUR

EQUINOX PUBLISHING (ASIA) PTE LTD
No 3. Shenton Way
#10-05 Shenton House
Singapore 068805

www.EquinoxPublishing.com

A Japanese Memoir of Sumatra, 1945-1946:
Love and Hatred in the Liberation War
by Takao Fusayama

ISBN 978-602-8397-19-3

First Equinox Edition 2010

Copyright © 1993 by Cornell Southeast Asia Program Publications; renewed 2010. This edition is authorized by the original publisher, Cornell Southeast Asia Program Publications.

Printed in the United States

1 3 5 7 9 10 8 6 4 2

All rights reserved. No part of this publication may be reproduced, stored in a retrieval system, or transmitted in any form or by any means, electronic, mechanical, photocopying, recording or otherwise without the prior permission of Equinox Publishing.

Table of Contents

	Page
Editorial Note..	7
Introduction by Saya Shiraishi.......................................	9
Author's Preface...	15
Chapter One — The End of World War II.......................	19
Chapter Two — Japan and Indonesia...............................	29
Chapter Three — The Start of the Independence War.......	37
Chapter Four — Prevention of a Japanese-Acehnese Battle....................	49
Chapter Five — To Riots in Medan...................................	59
Chapter Six — The Fifth Corps of the Youth Party..........	65
Chapter Seven — A Strategy of Anti-Japanese Agitation..	77
Chapter Eight — The Outbreak of the Tebing Incident....	93
Chapter Nine — The Story behind the Tebing Incident...	105
Chapter Ten — The Great National Moral Imperative...	125
Chapter Eleven — Japanese-Indonesian Friendship is Restored................	141
Chapter Twelve — Love and Hate......................................	157
Chapter Thirteen — The Distress of a Freedom Fighter.........	163
Chapter Fourteen — The Japanese Withdrawal from Aceh....	169
Chapter Fifteen — The Decline of the Fifth Corps............	175

Chapter Sixteen Leaving Medan...................................	193
Chapter Seventeen Hoping for Indonesian Success.............	201
Chapter Eighteen Indonesia after My Repatriation...........	213
Postscript...	227

Illustrations

Dr. Fusayama...	17
Map of Northern Sumatra..	21
Drawing: The Guerrilla Fighter.....................................	25
Siantar Hotel..	43
Governor Hasan in 1945...	52
Liaison Office at Lombok Avenue.................................	70
Fifth Corps Office at Lombok Avenue..........................	70
Tebing Tinggi: Central Square......................................	108
The Barracks of Capt. Iio's Troops near the Railway Station.....	108
Tebing Tinggi Railway Station......................................	108
Maj. Gen. Shunpo Sawamura..	130
Rebuilt Mosque at the End of Serdang Street...............	151
British Officer's Houses on Serdang Street...................	151
Drawing: A Freedom Fighter and his Lover Living in the RAPWI Camp...	164
Government Building and Conference Hall of Belawan City...	189
Amir Sjarifuddin, Colonel Tahir, and Lt. Colonel Sucipto........	203
Drawing: Belawan Harbor...	208
The Author in Front of the Lakeside Villa in Parapat where Sukarno and Hatta were Imprisoned............................	215
A Group of Freedom Fighters in Kota Raja.................	219
The Author with Ismed..	222
The Author with Nirwan...	222
Colonel Tahir, the Author, and Mr. Nip Xzrim, 1990	223

EDITORIAL NOTE

Dr. Takao Fusayama's memoir was first brought to our attention by Louis Allen, the well-known English historian of World War 2 and author of the classic account of the Allied victory in the Pacific, *End of the War in Asia*.[1] Dr. Fusayama, an eminent professor of dentistry in Tokyo, in his search to obtain a copy of Allen's book, then out of print, spent a couple of days with Louis Allen at his home in Durham in the northeast of England, about four years ago. Fusayama recounted his experiences as a signals officer in the Japan's Imperial Guard Division to Allen, who even persuaded his guest to talk over the telephone with one of the British officers who had interrogated him after Japan's surrender more than forty years earlier. While in Sumatra Fusayama had become involved with the Indonesian war of independence, and, as Allen wrote: "All this he has not only written up in Japanese, but he's produced a typescript, about 50,000 words, I reckon, on this period of the surrender and the various modus vivendi he and the other Japanese had to contrive in order to walk the tightrope between obeying the surrender orders to us and keeping the friendship of the locals whom they'd, in their view, liberated from the Dutch. It's an interesting document on this period, and he is an intelligent observer." Through the good offices of Dr. Peter Carey at Oxford, Louis Allen finally submitted Dr. Fusayama's memoir to Cornell Modern Indonesia Project, offering to write an introduction for it. Sadly, Allen died in December 1991, long before we were able to

---

1 London: Hart David, 1976. Among Allen's other books are: *Burma: The Longest War 1941-45* (London: Dent, 1984); *Japan the Years of Triumph: from Feudal Isolation to Pacific Empire* (New York: American Heritage Press, 1971); *Singapore 1941-1942* (London: David Poynter, 1977); *Sittang the Last Battle: The End of the Japanese in Burma, July-August 1945* (London: Macdonald, 1973).

prepare Dr. Fusayama's memoir for English publication. Instead, Dr. Saya Shiraishi, who is currently teaching at Cornell, has provided us with an interesting introduction from a historical perspective, throwing light on the importance of this memoir for an overall view of this period in the history of Japan and Indonesia. Dr. Shiraishi has herself researched and written on the Japanese occupation of Sumatra, and during the 1970s she interviewed many Japanese army veterans, both in Sumatra and Japan, who had participated in the occupation of Sumatra and its aftermath.

One of our chief reservations in publishing the memoir lay in the author's description of it as a "documentary novel," but we discovered that the "fictions" in the narrative relate mainly to Dr. Fusayama's dramatization of the action by putting into direct speech his memories of the general tenor of his conversations with some of the major protagonists. As he notes in his Preface, he recorded his recollections immediately after his repatriation to Japan, and it is evident that his rendition of the events he witnessed are true to his perceptions at the time. Dr. Fusayama has not changed the names of the major historical actors involved, and, as he reassured us:

> In reality fictional names were used only for Jusuf and his lover, Merry. Jusuf was killed in the war but his relatives are alive. Merry is also alive somewhere in Holland. Since Jusuf was suspected to be related with enemy, I do not like to embarrass them by disclosing the real names. This hiding will not affect the history because they did not play any significant role.

Dr. Fusayama's memoir offers an unusual and illuminating account of this period in Sumatra's history.

INTRODUCTION

I have three namelists in front of me which I acquired during the course of my research on the Japanese occupation of North Sumatra. They were composed by a former Japanese military officer in Medan, East Sumatra, and dated May 11, 1952. The title of the first list reads, in Japanese, "Namelist of the Japanese who died in battle or of illness in/around Medan." It contains 102 names, each with information concerning the person's "former military affiliation," "hometown" in Japan (one, however, is from Korea, one from Taiwan), and a brief record of how and where he died. A certain "Shimada," for example, "died during the fight against the Dutch in front of Siantar Railroad Station, July 27, 1947. An art college graduate, an excellent painter."

Three notes at the end of the list inform the reader that there are 88 additional Japanese who reportedly died in the region, among them the 83 who were massacred in Tebing Tinggi in December 1945 (see below, Chapter 8), but their names are unknown. There may have been further deaths which have not been confirmed. With the few exceptions of those who died of malaria or other illnesses, "most are martyrs to Indonesian independence who fell in battle against the Dutch."

All the deaths took place after August 15, 1945, the date marking the "end" of World War II for Japan. This record provides a basis for the claim that there were more Japanese casualties during Indonesia's revolutionary war than during Japan's three-and-a-half year occupation of the tropical land.

The second list contains 97 names of the "members of the Japanese Association in Medan." It provides such data as birth date, age, former military affiliation, family address in Japan, current address, marriage and children, current occupation. These men were living in Medan with their families (presumably Indonesian-born) as "mechanics," "automobile repairmen," "plantation clerks," "pharmacists," "blacksmiths," "*judo* instructors" etc. Their birth dates range from 1907 to 1923. When the list was prepared in 1952, they were 29 to 45 years old. Some had already lived in Sumatra for ten years since the Japanese landing in the island in 1942.

I was also told in interviews I conducted during my research that, in addition to the names listed here, there must be other Japanese who when they married entered the wives' families, becoming Muslims, acquiring Indonesian names, and being lost to their fellow Japanese. A few more names would then be mentioned of those who had come to the Dutch East Indies before World War II, had subsequently been recruited to serve in the Japanese occupation government, and then remained on in Indonesia which had apparently become their home.

The third list contains 20 names, with their family addresses in Japan, of people who in 1952 had just been sent back by ship to Japan from Medan.[1]

I met some of these returnees in Tokyo in 1974. One said that he was happy that he had been able to come back to Japan, had started life anew, and was planning to write a memoir after his retirement. Indeed, his book was published some years later. Another made it clear that he had been "forced" by the Indonesian government to leave the village in Aceh where he was farming. According to his old friends, he had close trusting relationships with the religious and political leaders in Aceh, among them the charismatic Tgk. Daud Beureueh who was to lead a revolt against the government in 1953. Two others did not want to talk about their experiences. They were working for the Japan-Indonesia petroleum trade and their "past" was currently both an asset and liability. It was not an "unforgettable, exotic" experience, but their life was still tied to it.

During the 1970s, large numbers of war-time memoirs were written

---

[1] The combined figure is significant enough considering the fact that by the end of World War II, (1) in the whole of Sumatra, there was only one division (Konoe-Daini Division) in the north and one brigade in the south; (2) due to the drastic reduction in the numbers of Japanese soldiers, the "division" barely managed to maintain its structure through incorporating the hastily organized *Giyu-gun* forces of local youths (at least 15 companies and 4 platoons in Aceh, 4 companies and 3 platoons in Medan) into its rank and file. See Saya Shiraishi, "Nihon Gunsei Ka no Aceh [Aceh under the Japanese Military Administration]" *Southeast Asia: History and Culture* [Tokyo] 5 (1975): 141.

and published in Japan. Among them, the "Indonesian experience" of sharing with young revolutionaries their historical moment (the period of the revolutionary war rather than Japan's occupation of the land) was remembered with unfading enthusiasm. The experience was something too significant for the veterans to let it vanish from their life. The Indonesian revolutionaries were young, and so were the Japanese. That period was as dear a memory of youth for the Japanese who had participated in the events as for the Indonesian youths themselves.

"Themselves"? Indeed, in most writings of "Indonesian" history, the "Japanese" have played the roles of peripheral characters -- either villains, such as ruthless *kenpeitai*, or sympathetic supporters of the nationalist cause. Japan's wartime policies were analyzed in the light of their effects on Indonesian national independence which was soon to follow. The fates of the Japanese after Japan's surrender to the Allies were viewed as insignificant episodes of this chaotic transitional period. The Japanese were, more or less, the actors assigned minor roles who failed to disappear promptly from the stage after the spotlight moved away from them.

These "Japanese soldiers" were, however, as we learn in this book, not professionally trained military men. The majority of them had been conscripted for the war, from their previous work places, such as offices, hospitals, factories, ricefields, shops, or schools, summoned by a single postcard sent out by the state, and subsequently "sent down" to a land of which they were supplied with little information.

Giving his "brief personal history," Takao Fusayama, the author of this memoir writes:

> He was born in Gifu Prefecture of Japan in 1916 and graduated from Tokyo Medical and Dental University in 1938 becoming a dentist. He was then called to army service and after studying at the Military Communication School for 8 months became an officer commanding a wireless platoon of the Divisional Communication Corps of the Imperial Guard Division.
>
> The division was mobilized in 1940 and he advanced through South China, Vietnam, Cambodia, Thailand, Malaya and Singapore and landed on the coast of Sumatra in 1942. He stayed mostly in Medan and later moved to Aceh becoming Communication Company Commander of the Fourth Imperial Guard Infantry Regiment as

Captain.

During his stay in Sumatra he studied the history and folklore of the Indonesian races as a hobby, becoming intimate with many Indonesian leaders.

In the land far away from home, these Japanese conscripts experienced, as their young Indonesian counterparts did, "in the most intimate way the collapse of the Dutch and Japanese colonial regimes."[2] It was, moreover, the state that had sent them down to Sumatra which collapsed. Fusayama writes:

> After surrending he was called to the Liaison Office in Medan by his Division to organize relations with the Indonesian Independence Movement.

Now the individual who "as a hobby" had studied the "history and folklore" of the land had to be called and asked to take charge. The era of personal adventures replaced that of the state's military rule. Though Fusayama did not intend to leave the military organization, which had apparently lost its centrally controlled line of command and was left to take care of itself locally, he still was not sure of the future course of events. "We, the Japanese soldiers, were quite pessimistic about repatriation. We were afraid that we would be detained in Sumatra for our whole lives...." [p. 136].

Years later, researchers in the field of Indonesian studies, whether their focus was the social revolution, the battles between the Indonesian and Dutch military forces, or the history of national independence, would interview the repatriated Japanese as informants who had been present as third-party eye-witnesses, who could supply supplemental data and perspectives on the events that had taken place among the Indonesian social forces.

Some of the Japanese, however, could not help boasting, after 30 years, of how "much" they had "contributed" to their brothers' independence.

---

2 Benedict Anderson, "Old State, New Society," in his *Language and Power* (Ithaca: Cornell University Press, 1990), p. 111.

Some, on the other hand, would modestly disclaim any significance in the "part" they played in the "independence" war against the Dutch. The exciting adventure stories of these "informants" which were viewed merely as "self" serving have largely been left in the researchers' notebooks without finding a place in print, if they were ever, in fact, even written down during the interviews, and the informants' modesty was respectfully accepted as such. In the national history of Indonesia, who would care about the pride, dream, desperation, love, pleasure, hatred, or death of any young individual "Japanese"?

These interviews, nevertheless, encouraged the ex-soldiers to write their memoirs, at the same time, however, offering the historical context of their experiences. The momentary separation between the state and their individual lives, which in fact allowed those Japanese whose names appear in the three lists to choose their own course of action, largely disappeared in their conscious choice of words.

Yet, the readers of this "documentary novel" written by Takao Fusayama will perceive the zeal with which his story is narrated. It is also his dedication that has brought his recollections across the Pacific. He not only published his memoir in Japanese, but also took the pains to translate it into English himself and search for an English-speaking audience. This unceasing commitment to the memory of the brief period of their youth, during which the lives of some hundreds of Japanese young men actually did change, is the notable feature shared by other memoirs as well. Behind their narratives we find this zeal for life. It is there, because it was their own life. Their own youth. We hear in this book, the voice of hundreds of youths whose "personal" life-stories in a "foreign" land have been edited away.

It is through this voice, however, that we may come closer to understanding the nature of the revolutionary war and the "stateless youth"[3] who fought it. One of the former Japanese "deserters"[!] once answered my question as to why he had not returned home, "Oh, it was just natural for me to stay there." He did not choose to be sent to Sumatra as he did not choose to be born a Japanese. He found, nevertheless, that his life should belong to Sumatra whose natural beauty he loved dearly.

---

3 Anderson, "Old State, New Society," p. 94.

He had had enough of the military, enough of the state's arbitrary control over his life. He had never forgiven the state, Japan, that had intruded into his life and, upon his graduating from college, sent him out to the warfront. He was a revolutionary youth "himself."

His story is yet to be written. Takao Fusayama's account of his own experiences, however, will open up and invite more attention to this unexplored field.

> "Shima: Died while producing hand-grenades in Karaishi Plantation in Aceh on February, 23, 1948. Buried with an official Indonesian military funeral in the Town of Perelak with respect and care.... Well trusted and loved among Aceh's leaders."
>
> "Suzuki: April '46. Murdered by a native (he [Suzuki] was a fat, big man)
>
> "Hayashi: Feb. 1, '46. Committed suicide with a pistol at 10:30 in the morning (cause unknown)....

Saya Shiraishi
Cornell University
February 1993

AUTHOR'S PREFACE

When World War II ended, I surrendered as a young officer of the 2nd Imperial Guard Division of the Japanese army in Sumatra, Indonesia. The Allied Forces of British-Indian and Dutch troops landed on Sumatra as the almighty victor. As Indonesians proclaimed their independence and began their fight for freedom, the Allied Forces strictly prohibited the Japanese from assisting Indonesian independence. We Japanese, who had advanced south holding high the flag of Asian liberation, could only observe the lonely fight by the Indonesians. Furthermore, we were threatened by the fear of being forced to fight against the beloved Indonesians. Although the Allied Forces did not directly order us to fight, various orders and strategies indirectly pushed us in that direction. Any confusion could immediately cause an unfortunate conflict with our brothers.

Under such circumstances, I was appointed to the position of liaison officer managing Indonesian affairs for the Japanese army in North Sumatra, because I had many close friends among the Indonesians. I devoted all my youthful energy to preventing or settling conflicts between Indonesians and Japanese. Through this effort, I personally observed the meshing of love and hatred by the people involved in the historic events, which were indeed stranger than fiction.

When I was repatriated to Japan, I immediately recorded this emotional history before my memory faded. Its publication was, however, deferred because my sympathetic efforts in behalf of Indonesian independence transgressed the orders of the victors, and I thus feared being accused of war crimes. More than thirty years passed during which I was absorbed in the academic demands of my proper career field. In 1979 I was invited by the Freedom Fighters Veterans Council in Medan Area, supported by the North Sumatra Government, to spend a delightful week there because of my contribution to Indonesian independence. Thus encouraged, I published a book in Japanese in 1981, adding dates and names from various sources for increased documentary accuracy. I further translated the volume into English and presented it to Mr. Louis Allen in England who kindly introduced it to Cornell University. It is my extreme pleasure that this memoir is being published by the University's Modern Indonesia Project.

This book is a documentary novel describing the dramatic events of those early months of Indonesian independence. The descriptions which follow are substantially based on fact, but some details are illustrated by complementary fictions. False names were used in some places so as not to embarrass the relevant people. I would be more than grateful if readers appreciate this frank account of human behavior that occurred during such a great turning point in national and international history.

Dr. Takao Fusayama, 1988

Captain Fusayama, 1945

CHAPTER ONE
THE END OF WORLD WAR II

MOVING TO TINJUWAN ESTATE

It was late September 1945. We were silently hoeing the ground under the burning rays of the bright, tropical sun. The earth was covered with a threatening silence with no birds singing and no wind stirring. With our sweat streaming down, we were hoeing the earth merely to survive in the interior of Sumatra, several thousand kilometers from our fatherland, as a defeated people over whom the victor held the power of life and death.

A month previously, on August 15, the Pacific War on which Japan had embarked to determine the fate of Asia, had ended with the Allies achieving their merciless goal of Japan's unconditional surrender. The surrender agreement was reached in Rangoon, Burma, between the Southeast Asia Command of Allied Forces and the Southern General Command of Japanese Forces. Our Imperial Guard Division defending northern Sumatra received the order to surrender from 25th Army headquarters in central Sumatra. Under the divisional order, in mid-September our 4th Imperial Guard Infantry Regiment defending the coast of northern Aceh Province, moved to the Tinjuwan Estate in the interior of East Sumatra Province, leaving small units of troops in the principal towns for the security of the administrators there.

Knowing nothing of our future fate, we, the defeated, began to reclaim the superannuated plantation of fallen oil palms to grow vegetables for our survival. When we first gathered here, we could eat only a small amount of rice and powdered soy beans due to the Allied Forces strict restriction of the food supply. We therefore hurried to cultivate vegetables, while temporarily soothing our hunger with wild water grasses collected from streams. Fortunately, in Sumatra vegetables grow surprisingly fast. Only one week after planting the shoots of a vegetable with heavy leaves, called *koroko*, on the farm, we were able to eat part of the leaves cooked in the soy bean soup. Meanwhile, we learned to pick clams on the seashore of the nearby fishing port, Tanjung Tiram, and they became an important source of protein for us. We gradually began to recover from the collapse we had experienced immediately after we had moved, completely dispirited, from Aceh Province to this estate.

We thus spent one month immersed in the effort of producing food within this estate, completely isolated from the external world. The news from the Domei News Service then began to be delivered. It told us of the conditions in our fatherland, occupied by foreign armies for the first time in its history. Starvation was even worse there than here. At that time, I was the commander of the Regimental Communications Company. In order to give my officers and soldiers motivation to live, I told them the following:

> Our fatherland has been completely destroyed by the war. The Japanese remaining in Japan are only weak old people, women, and children. For the economic reconstruction of our fatherland we, young men in the prime of life, now staying abroad, must return to help them. Although we do not know when we will be repatriated, let us keep ourselves healthy and increase our abilities as much as possible before repatriation so as to be able to work effectively when we return to our homeland. That is our duty to our nation.

I began a lecture course in our barracks to prepare for our social life in Japan, lecturing every day for three hours after the siesta, while farming in the morning. A graduate from an agricultural school lectured on agriculture and practical training in farming during the mornings. A graduate from a school of commerce taught finance and book keeping. I myself taught English and occasionally gave news commentaries. Although the Domei News Service informed us that Dr. Sukarno had proclaimed Indonesian independence in Java, it sounded to us, who were farming outside of the real world, as faint news from another world, that had no relevance for us.

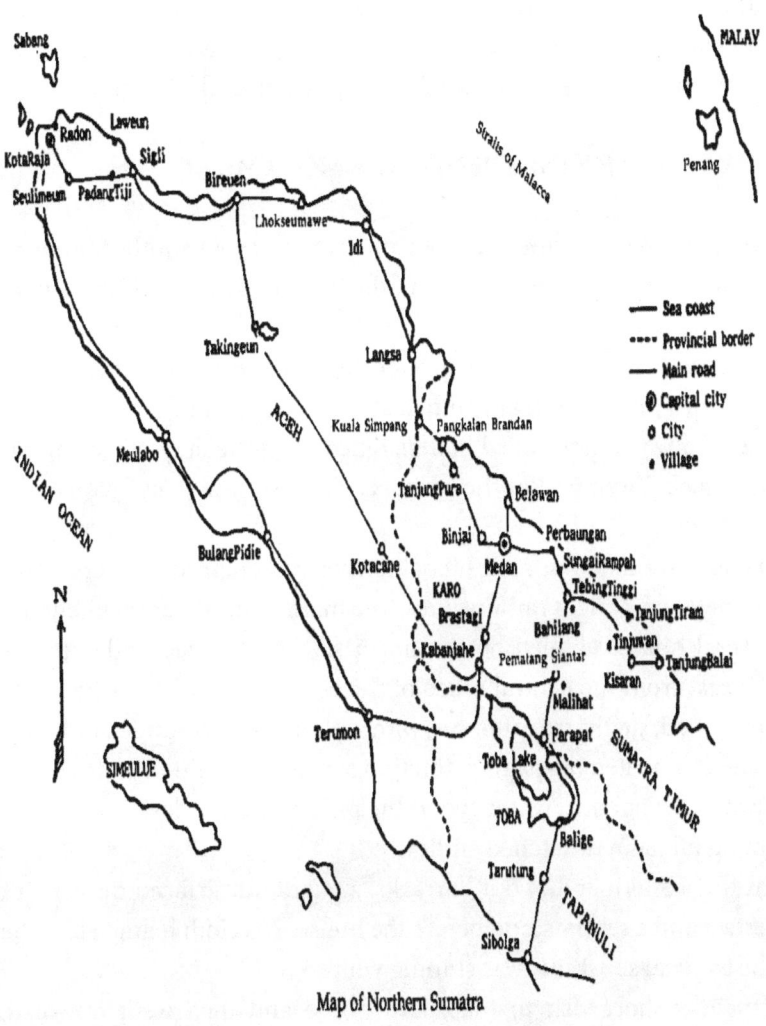

Map of Northern Sumatra

In October, we heard that the independence movement had also started in Sumatra and that the government of independent Indonesia had been founded in Medan, the capital of Sumatra. But we saw no signs of it on this estate. The 2,000 farm laborers called *orang kontrak* (contract coolies), though they surely knew that Japan was defeated, continued to work under the control of Japanese managers without any change in attitude, going to farm every day in groups of some fifty men.

ARRIVAL OF THE INDEPENDENCE MOVEMENT

It was about the middle of October, after we had spent another two weeks on Tinjuwan Estate, that the wave of the independence movement finally reached this calm, isolated estate.

As usual, I was hoeing the ground together with my soldiers during the morning, and then taking lunch after washing off my sweat using the native cold water bath called *mandi*. Since I was the duty officer-in-chief for the week, I went out of the barracks on patrol while my soldiers were taking their nap.

Tinjuwan Estate was a big oil palm farm, 30 square kilometers in area, with a network of light railway lines. The main force of our regiment lived in several houses aligned on the north side of the road and extending to the east from the central office of the estate. The houses were square, white-walled, single-story houses, with wide lawns surrounded by hedges. The superannuated oil-palm plantation spreading behind the houses was cultivated for our survival. Beyond the plantation, the dark green woods of young oil palms stretched endlessly.

At the western end of our barracks, a guard house faced the center of the estate and a sentry stood before the house. His cloth helmet, bleached by the tropical sunshine, was shining white.

I paid a short visit to the guard house and then went out of the camp, returning the sentry's salute as he presented arms. Next, I visited the telephone exchange in the estate office to express appreciation to my soldiers working there, and then continued on. Behind the office was a locomotive shed for the light railway and a huge factory for oil manufacturing and rice cleaning. Further down to the west, several gigantic collective dwellings called *pondok* stood in a line, their huge brown roofs rising high between the tops of the coconut palms. A big meeting hall roofed with nipa leaves was in the middle of the line.

Passing by the hall, I was surprised to find an unusual meeting being held there. The speakers were the youth party leaders who had come from Medan for the independence campaign. Numerous brown skinned bodies were milling around in the sultry air of the hall and bloodshot eyes tensely watched the stage. The speaker's fierce voice mingled with the atmosphere, which, heated by the audience and the excitement, seemed to burn as fiercely as the sunshine outside.

As I loved speaking the Indonesian language, I easily made Indonesian friends everywhere. Since most clerks and the leading workers of the estate were my friends, I stopped to observe the meeting, exchanging smiles with the people there.

A long, simple wooden table had been placed on the stage. There sat the leaders of the youth party from Medan, together with the leading members of the estate, their faces shining with tension. The earthen floor was packed with seated onlookers surrounded by human walls. A number of curious children dancing about at the entrances also watched the stage. An intrepid-looking brown man on the stage was speaking and shaking his fist. "For three hundred and fifty years until the Japanese forces came, we lived miserable lives under the Dutch repression. Look at our Sumatra, where palm trees cover the earth to the horizon. But where did the fruits fall? They fell not on Sumatra but all on the Netherlands."

A storm of applause rose from the audience. The speaker on the stage spoke again, holding his right hand high like Adolf Hitler, the German dictator:

Sumatra has many excellent oil fields. However, where did the pipes open? Dear comrades! They all opened in the Netherlands. Now, we must stand up. We must take back our property into our own hands. Gentlemen. You must stand up for the liberation of your fatherland. Let us unite all Indonesians and risk our lives in the battle. Seizing every possible weapon, let us now prepare for the freedom war. All Indonesians must be fighters. All hundred million Indonesians must fight as one unit.

The speech was surprisingly good. The response was tremendous. The speaker, shaking his hair and scattering his sweat, holding his fist high, continued his speech, asking the audience for answers as he made each essential point.

"Dear comrades! Are you afraid of death?"

The audience answered in unison, like a thousand claps of thunder.

"*Tidak* (No)!"

"Then let us cry aloud. *Merdeka atau Mati* [Freedom or Death]!"

In response to the cry of the speaker, the whole audience cried back together, holding their fists high.

The meeting was over. The conclusion was reached. The audience, who had cried aloud, streamed out of the hall like a whirling muddy stream. My heart was full of emotion, floating on that stream.

AN EMOTIONAL NIGHT

History was now streaming. It was actually leaping. While we Japanese had abandoned the war and were silently farming on this estate several thousands of kilometers away from our home country, the Indonesian people stood up to build a new history with their own hands. I was confounded by the fact that the dream of Indonesian independence, which we Japanese had desired but sadly failed to achieve, began to become real, irrespective of the Japanese. My heart was mercilessly broken by feeling the powerlessness of being one of the defeated, kicked out of the real world of history. Some time ago I had heard the news of Indonesian independence but it was merely distant news. But, today I felt deep pity for myself, returning alone to my barracks with nothing to do, after seeing the real historical movement in front of my eyes.

In the late evening of that day, however, the leaders of the freedom campaign from Medan stealthily visited my residence, led there by the chief clerk of the estate. Admitting them into the officers' dining room, I listened greedily to their story of the independence movement. They told me that the governor of independent Sumatra was Teuku Moehammad Hasan, an Acehnese who used to be the deputy mayor of Medan under the Japanese administration. Through my study of Acehnese folklore he had become an intimate personal friend, and I had often visited his private residence. His deputy, the assistant governor, was Maharaja Soankupon Siregar, a senior Batak leader who used to be chairman of the Provincial People's Congress. I had often visited his house too, to study Batak folklore and was welcomed there as if I were a relative. Hearing this news, the dream of the independence movement suddenly began to course through my heart, warming my blood. The freedom fighters from various parties were risking their lives to raise the national flag of independence in Medan. I had so far been hearing about the movement as if it were a story from another distant world, since I had been living the life of a hermit, as described in China, *seiko-udoku* (farming when clear and reading when rainy). However, the movement of the real world was now almost touching my skin.

The Guerrilla Fighter

Sitting around me, the campaign leaders discussed policies for obtaining independence with both youthful passion and wisdom, and repeatedly asked for my opinion. In response to their request, I stressed most strongly that they should concentrate on the Dutch as their enemy. I argued as follows:

> When we Japanese soldiers landed on Sumatra, the power of the resisting Dutch army was as absurd as the battle play of children. Although I do not know how the Dutch army was trained thereafter in Europe, the military power of such a small country, which was occupied for a long time by Germany, is likely to be very weak. The British army is, however, quite different. Although they were helped by the Americans, they, anyhow, defeated the Japanese. In reality, their resistance was not inconsiderable when we fought in Malaya and Singapore. There would be little chance for you if you challenged them directly and frontally. Fortunately, Sumatra is not a British colony. Distinguishing the Dutch from the British, you should fight tenaciously until you finally succeed, being neither hasty nor negligent.
>
> I have studied the history of the Dutch conquest of Sumatra. The Acehnese people were able to resist Dutch aggression for as long as thirty years, with weapons no more substantial than traditional spears and bows. The Indonesian people, who were split at that time, are now tightly united. The military ability of Indonesians who were trained by the Japanese as volunteer soldiers is incomparably stronger than in previous times. If you fight cleverly, the chance of victory is not necessarily unattainable. If all European countries ally with the Dutch, however, immediate and full independence might not be possible and you might be compelled to compromise in a federation with the Dutch. Even in this case, however, you must keep your military and diplomatic rights in your hand. If you give up these rights, your independence will be invalid.

Although I was neither a politician nor strategist, I expressed my opinion as thoughtfully as possible in response to their enthusiasm. They continued their earnest discussions with bright eyes until they retired very late, shaking my hand with many thanks.

This was really a night of extreme emotion that heated my young blood. When I recovered my senses after seeing them off, however, I felt depressed again. I expected that my life would probably continue to be one of mere subsistence agriculture, excluded from the events of world history. Thereafter, however, bit by bit, pieces of information about the independence movement in Sumatra began to reach my ears.

CHAPTER TWO
JAPAN AND INDONESIA

HOLY ARMY FOR ASIAN LIBERATION

I believe that the Japanese and Indonesians have been brothers for 2,000 years. It is said that the Proto-Malaysians came some 4,000 years ago from the central part of Asia to the south, forming the Malayan race on the Malay Peninsula and then crossed the Malacca Straits to Sumatra. They then spread to Java, Kalimantan, and Sulawesi, forming the races collectively known now as Indonesians. They went further north forming the Filipinos and the Formosan native tribe in Taiwan. Some 2,000 years ago, they finally reached Japan and formed the Japanese race mixing with the people from the continent. Part of the blood of the Japanese is, therefore, Malaysian, that is, Indonesian.

Indonesian people recognized the presence of Japan for the first time during the Japanese-Russian War. Although the Dutch governed the Sunda Archipelago for 350 years, the Acehnese people at the northern end of Sumatra continued the desperate fight against the Dutch, who intended to conquer the whole area, until early this century when the Japanese-Russian War occurred. The Acehnese sultan was supported in his resistance by the Acehnese people, who did not fear death in their holy war to defend Islam. However, reaching the limit of his strength the sultan finally surrendered in 1904.

The triumphant Dutch forces commanded by Colonel Van Dalen pushed further into the Takingeun Highlands and advanced up the valley between the Barisan Mountains, using hired African soldiers armed with modern rifles and elephants. Reaching the Batak Highlands, they fiercely attacked the Batak people with massacre, arson, plunder, and rape. When Singa Mangaraja who commanded the Batak people was killed in the

Toba district in 1907, the occupation of the whole of Indonesia by the Dutch was complete.

The Japanese-Russian War was fought in 1904-5, just when the Indonesians were fighting their last desperate war. The Russian Baltic Fleet, which was sent to destroy Japan, passed eastwards through the Malacca Straits, spreading across the entire width of the strait. Because the Indonesians in Sumatra could do nothing when shelled by a single destroyer from the Dutch navy, they thought it was the end of Japan when they saw the great Baltic Fleet of gigantic warships with huge guns.

When they heard that this fleet was completely destroyed by the Japanese navy and that the Russian army was driven out of Korea and Manchuria by the Japanese army, they began to expect that Japan would liberate Asia. Since this expectation could not be openly expressed, they spread it secretly through the old Joyoboyo myth which said that a yellow giant would soon come from the north to liberate the people.

In 1941, only 36 years later, the Pacific War broke out. Japanese forces began to march south advocating a holy war for Asian liberation. Their army marched from French Indochina through Thailand into Malaya. The Malayans, who were of the same race as the Indonesians, cooperated with the Japanese enthusiastically. The Fujiwara Agency of the Japanese army called for Asian liberation from the radio station of Penang as soon as they occupied the island. Indonesians in Sumatra, just across from Penang, were delighted, appreciating that the yellow giant was finally approaching.

Said Abu Bakar, a young leader of the brave Acehnese race could not stay still and crossed the Malacca Strait to Penang in a small boat with a few comrades to contact the agent commander, Major Fujiwara. Said Abu Bakar was enraptured on hearing that the Japanese would soon advance to Sumatra, and he returned home to prepare for their coming. He organized cooperators from within PUSA, a religious youth party in Aceh. Wearing jackets with the F-mark inside their collar, the cooperators rapidly spread along the northern coast of Sumatra like a fire burning a dry field. The explosives the Dutch had placed under bridges everywhere for defense against the Japanese were removed by Abu Bakar's followers. They incited riots, cut telephone cables, and even attacked the Dutch barracks. Our Imperial Guard Division landed on Sumatra under such conditions.

Our Imperial Guard Division occupied Singapore, the stronghold of European colonial occupation in the Far East, on February 15, 1942, then landed at several places on the northern coast of Sumatra before dawn on March 12. I myself landed on the coast of Tanjung Tiram as a wireless platoon commander following the division headquarters. The Dutch defense force had fled the coast. The inhabitants hung makeshift flags of the rising sun in front of their houses and flocked to the coast to welcome our holy army and assist our landing. Immediately on landing, we hurried on to attack the fleeing Dutch army, pursuing it for a week until we reached Padang, a port on the Indian Ocean coast. Cornered there, the Dutch army surrendered.

Our unit was the well-known Imperial Guard Division. Soldiers were well-disciplined and soon became friends with the inhabitants. They particularly loved children since they had left their own children in Japan. Returning smiles for smiles, we enjoyed the brotherhood that had originated some 2,000 years ago.

MY FOLKLORE STUDY

Thereafter, we enjoyed three and a half years living as the occupying force surrounded by inhabitants who were very sympathetic to us. Although the soldiers on overseas expeditions were very busy during the fighting, they usually had considerable spare time when they stayed in a place after the end of a battle. It was usual for them to kill time by drinking, visiting prostitutes, and other amusements. I, however, was interested in the folklore of various Indonesian tribes and began to spend my spare time studying.

When I went to the Batak Highlands in pursuit of the enemy, I was surprised to find huge houses with steep raftered roofs in the cool green woods, that looked so similar to the huge dwellings of the Shirakawago Village of Hida in Japan. I was told that the people lived in an extended family system similar to the families of Shirakawago. More than 1,000 meters high, the Batak Highlands were cool like our autumn, all four seasons, even though they were right on the equator, and the Batak people had kept their phantasmic old customs from 1,000 years ago, living a life of earthly paradise isolated from the world below.

Their history since the birth of their tribe was written in Batak characters on the bark skins of big trunks. They had myths very similar to the Japanese. Their ancestor was also said to have lived above the Plain of Heaven. There was a dreamingly beautiful inland sea, Toba Lake. A peak rising close to its south shore was called Pusuk Bukit. Like the Japanese ancestor named Niniginomikoto, who descended from Heaven onto the summit of Takachiho in Hyuga, the Batak ancestor named Si Boru Deakparjar descended onto Pusuk Bukit. I was absorbed in the study of the Batak people as if I was possessed by some mystical spirit. Fortunately, I was a wireless platoon commander of the divisional communications troop and was free to travel throughout the whole of Sumatra for my research on the pretext of inspecting the wireless stations under my control. After reading literature borrowed from the Medan Library, I visited educated Indonesians who understood English or German and obtained much information and materials from them. (The result of this study was published by the Kaizo Pub. Co. in 1975 under the title, "Mystical Batak People.")

Close to my residence in Medan, there lived a Batak family named Pulungan. Various Batak youths often visited this house because there were two pretty daughters and three handsome sons in the family. Ismed and Nirwan were among the visitors. When I mentioned my study, Ismed said "Those kinds of matters are well known to my uncle, Nirwan's father."

They introduced me to Maharaja Soankupon Siregar, who later became chairman of the Provincial People's Congress that was established by the Japanese military administration to prepare for Indonesian independence. He was a senior leader from a Batak royal family with the title of Maharaja (Great King). He was very happy with my study and extended all possible assistance to me, welcoming me as if I were a member of his family.

He kindly introduced me to many other Indonesian leaders and scholars and I also became close friends of the young people in their families through frequent visits. Though their religion did not permit drinking alcohol, they often asked me to go drinking with them.

The restaurants we visited were, however, not for hard liquor. They were outdoor restaurants under green trees serving coffee. Although Sumatra was very warm in the daytime, it was fairly cool and comfortable in the evening. Wearing a white polo shirt and white trousers instead of my military uniform, I often went cycling with them in the evenings. They and I were "drinking companions," going to drink coffee together.

Through this companionship, I rapidly mastered Indonesian conversation. They enjoyed talking with me, an Indonesian-speaking Japanese officer, friendly without reserve. Visiting families with them, I made many friends not only among the boys but also the girls. The girls nicknamed me "Sheiky" because they thought I looked like an Arabian sheik. My life in Medan was thus as pleasant as if I were already released from army service.

In 1943, I was temporarily appointed to the position of deputy-commander of the communications company of the 4th Imperial Guard Infantry Regiment and spent a year on the coast of Aceh. Living there, I began to study Acehnese folklore and became acquainted with Tuanku Mahmud, the grandson of the last Sultan of Aceh. He told me in detail the history of the Acehnese Kingdom in its golden age, and its downfall. I enjoyed listening to him at his humble palace called Rumah Aceh, every time I was in Kota Raja.

After I returned to Medan, I continued to study Aceh and became acquainted with Teuku Mr. Moehammad Hasan, the current Sumatran governor of independent Indonesia. He was born to an Ulebalang (middle ruling class) family in Sigli, North Aceh. He once studied law in the Netherlands and obtained the title of Meester (Master in English). When I first met him, he was the deputy mayor of Medan, expecting to be appointed mayor when Indonesia became independent.

TRAINING THE INDONESIAN SOLDIERS

In 1943 the American counter-attack started at Guadalcanal Island and the situation gradually worsened for the Japanese. The Japanese army established a new Indonesian army called *Giyugun* (the Volunteer Indonesian Army) and gave military training to the youths who volunteered. Another system of *Heiho* (military auxiliaries) who worked with Japanese forces as auxiliaries was also established. Many Indonesian young men willingly applied for it to defend their fatherland. Intelligent youths, selected from among them, were trained to be officers to lead the future Indonesian national forces. They endured the hard training by the Japanese army, their hearts burning with the mission to defend their fatherland and dreamt of Indonesian independence in the near future.

On my return from Aceh to the divisional communications troop in

Medan, I did not return to my post as wireless platoon commander, but instead, was made responsible for training new Japanese soldiers sent from Japan to various divisions for wireless communication. The shortage of wireless operators was a serious problem for the entire Japanese army in the south. At the same time, I also educated sixty Heiho allocated to our troops. Although this was the first experience of a collective lifestyle for the Indonesian youths, they diligently accepted our hard training, proud to be soldiers in uniform. Although my Indonesian language was not so fluent, they eagerly listened to my lectures on Indonesian national history without ever dozing. Their response was more serious than I expected and at times even astonished me.

THE JAPANESE ARMY SURRENDERS

In July 1945, I was reappointed to my position in Aceh and left Medan. This time, I was the regular communication company commander instead of deputy. A few weeks later, however, the atomic bombs fell on Hiroshima and Nagasaki, and Japan surrendered on August 15, 1945.

I learnt of the surrender several days later when I happened to be in Medan on a business trip. I hurriedly left Medan for Aceh and drove 500 kilometers through the day and night. Immediately on my arrival at Seulimeum where our regiment was stationed, I knocked at the door of the regiment commander and advised him to concentrate all the small units scattered along the coast and build fortresses. This was because I was afraid of riots by the Acehnese people, famous for their roughness, when they learnt of the Japanese defeat. In the last part of the war, excessive issuing of military currency seriously distressed the inhabitants by causing inflation, because the import of goods from Japan had been choked off by the Allied Forces. The Japanese army in their haste to build fortresses, ordered the inhabitants to cooperate and slapped the laborers when they were considered lazy. In addition, many coconut trees, which were important possessions of the local people, were cut down to build the seashore barricade. I knew well how bitter this was to the inhabitants.

However, when the people were actually informed of the Japanese surrender, my anxiety turned out to be mere fancy. The volunteer and auxiliary Indonesian soldiers, who had been working together with the Japanese, deeply grieved with the Japanese soldiers. The auxiliary soldiers of my company tearfully pleaded with their teacher, "Don't you remember? You Japanese told us to defend Sumatra till the last soldier. Why do you surrender? If you surrender, what will be our fate? Please let us continue to fight, even if it is Sumatra alone." Crying, they refused to be disbanded. The sergeant who was their teacher desperately persuaded them by saying, "Our Emperor, *Tennoheika*, ordered us to surrender. The Emperor's order is absolute to us. Please, please understand." And he himself began to cry.

Contrary to my expectation, no change occurred in the people's attitude toward us Japanese, in spite of our defeat. My comrade, Captain Kobayashi, who stayed in command of his company in the small village of Radon in northern Aceh, told me a story. When his company burnt down their temporary barracks and lined up in a row by the trucks, the village head formed a line with his people along the roadside and saw them off in tears. They genuinely grieved that Japan was defeated and appreciated that Japanese soldiers had worked harder than they to defend their fatherland. They understood that the hard work they were forced to perform by the Japanese army was all for their sake, and they expressed no grudge. Similar stories were told by almost all the troops withdrawing from the coastal fortresses.

The attitude of the people in the towns was similar. When I went to a movie theater, the ticket man, who was acquainted with me, kindly admitted me for no charge saying, "I feel sorry for you, the defeated Japanese. You don't have to pay. Just come in."

They were heartily sympathetic toward us, not minding the fact that they had seriously suffered from the heavy inflation caused by the excessive issuing of military currency.

In such an atmosphere, our 4th Imperial Guard Infantry Regiment took the train for Tinjuwan, leaving small units behind in the principal towns to protect the officials. On the Acehnese train, which had become very bumpy due to the lack of spare parts, we left Aceh, not knowing what our fate would be tomorrow. Passing through the dear city of Medan where I had spent most of my wartime life, we gathered at Tinjuwan Estate which was far inland, isolated from the outside world. We began to farm on the estate.

On this estate, too, all the Indonesian farmers were quite friendly and obedient to the Japanese and there was no disquieting atmosphere. The farmers' attitude showed hardly any sign of the Japanese defeat, though we were sure they knew of it.

CHAPTER THREE
THE START OF THE INDEPENDENCE WAR

PROCLAMATION OF INDONESIAN INDEPENDENCE

In contrast to the quiet in Sumatra, turbulent changes were occurring in Java, the main island of Indonesia, immediately following the Japanese surrender.

When the Japanese forces occupied Indonesia in 1942, the Japanese navy founded two schools for training young Indonesian leaders for independence. Dr. Sukarno was school master of one in Jakarta under the care of the naval liaison office headed by Rear Admiral Tadashi Maeda. Dr. Samsi was school master of a second in Surabaya under the care of Lt. Kazuyuki Mike, a paymaster for the 2nd South Expeditionary Fleet.

In September 1944, General K. Koiso, who had been stressing the necessity of Indonesian liberation since the prewar period, became the prime minister of Japan and ordered preparation for independence. In January 1945, the Independence Committee of Indonesia was formed, with Sukarno as chairman and Teuku M. Hasan representing Sumatra. They had planned to proclaim independence on September 7 but Japan surrendered on August 15, three weeks earlier than the scheduled proclamation.

They were immediately informed of the news of the Japanese surrender by a wireless operator in the Domei News Service. Sukarno and Hatta called the Independence Committee together at the official residence of Rear Admiral Maeda with his secret support. The committee then made the historic Proclamation of Independence on August 17 at 2 A.M., as follows:

Our Indonesian Nation herewith proclaims the Independence of

Indonesia. The transfer of sovereignty and other matters must be performed carefully and quickly. Jakarta, August 17th, 05. Sukarno and Hatta.

The 05 meant 2605 of the Japanese traditional calendar. The proclamation was written on naval letter paper, printed at the naval liaison office, and scattered by the youths using a navy car. It was broadcast to Indonesia by Radio Jakarta and to the world by the short wave radio of Domei News Service. The independence government established its first cabinet on August 29.

On September 8, the advance officer of the British army descended by parachute to the Jakarta airport and the British fleet entered the port of Jakarta on the 15th. According to Allied Forces' orders, the 16th Army Commander of Japan had announced a prohibition of public assemblies. Several hundred thousand people, however, gathered in the center of Jakarta singing the national song "Indonesian Raya" and Sukarno gave an historic public speech. The Japanese army looked on without intervening.

ARMING THE INDONESIAN FORCES

The Allied Forces began a full-scale advance on Indonesia by the end of September. Three British-Indian divisions commanded by Lt. Gen. Sir Phillip Christison advanced to Indonesia, with two divisions allocated to Java and one division to Sumatra. Before leaving Singapore for Indonesia, Christison declared that his army was landing in Indonesia only for the purpose of disarming the Japanese and had no desire to intervene in the domestic affairs of the Dutch East Indies.

The 2nd Southern Expeditionary Fleet of the Japanese navy commanded by Vice Admiral Yaichiro Shibata and the Mixed Defense Brigade of the Japanese army commanded by Major General Shigeo Iwabe were stationed in Surabaya. They were caught in a serious dilemma between their wish to hand over their arms to Indonesians and the prohibition by the Allied Forces. Fortunately, something happened to resolve their dilemma. On September 21, a Dutch advance officer, Captain Huijer, unexpectedly landed in Surabaya accompanied by only a few soldiers. Displaying his authority as the victor, he defiantly ordered the Japanese commanders to surrender to him immediately and to leave their arms under the guard of the Indonesian authorities until the Allied Forces took them over. Because Captain Huijer used to live in Surabaya, he thought that most Indonesians would be obedient to the Dutch when they returned, just like before. He did not know that the attitude of the Indonesian people had completely changed during the Japanese occupation.

When the Indonesians rushed to the Japanese barracks, Vice Admiral Shibata and Major General Iwabe ordered their soldiers to hand over all arms without resisting, explaining that in obeying the orders of Captain Huijer, the Japanese forces were to disarm themselves, leaving their weapons in the care of the Indonesians until the Allied Forces received them. The Indonesians thus obtained 26,000 rifles, 600 machine guns, cannons, anti-aircraft guns, and other weapons in the space of a few days. A large amount of war funds were also secretly given to the Indonesians by a naval paymaster, Lt. Kazuyuki Mike. A great Indonesian military power was thus established for the first time.

THE FIRST INDONESIAN VICTORY

On October 5, President Sukarno announced the foundation of his public security force, Tentera Keamanan Rakyat (TKR) and steadily expanded the army by gathering together the former volunteer and auxiliary soldiers trained by the Japanese. Ten divisions in Java and six in Sumatra were organized.

On October 26, the 49th British-Indian Brigade of 5,000 landed in Surabaya. The Indonesian force in Surabaya, who were well-armed with Japanese weapons, resolutely risked a night attack taught by the Japanese and completely destroyed the brigade, killing the commander. In early November, the British forces made an all-out counterattack on Surabaya, with one complete division of 24,000 and the support of shelling from warships and bombing from airplanes. Indonesian anti-aircraft guns given by the Japanese shot down three of the planes. The street fighting continued until November 12. The Indonesians tenaciously continued to resist with the song of "Merdeka atau Mati [Freedom or Death]" blaring through loud speakers. The spirits of the Indonesian forces were considerably raised by the initial victory and the independence war front extended throughout the whole of Java, and further, on to Sumatra and the other islands.

The Dutch political operation to recover their colony was carried out by van Mook, former vice-governor of the Dutch East Indies, who landed in Jakarta on October 5. He established an organization called the Netherlands Indies Civil Administration (NICA) and condemned the independent Republic of Indonesia as a Japanese-made dictatorial government. He also intended to re-establish the colonial government, and he approached senior members of various organizations through those who were educated as youths in the Netherlands. After unexpectedly encountering rejections, NICA turned into an intelligence agency aimed at undermining the solidarity of the independence movement.

PROCLAMATION OF INDEPENDENCE IN SUMATRA

Let me return to the story in Sumatra. There, too, the advance reconnaissance team descended by parachute on Polonia Airport in Medan on September 8. Nothing happened for a while. When the obedient surrender of the Imperial Guard Division of Japan had been confirmed by the reconnaissance, the preparatory advance unit of the Allied Forces landed at the airport several days later in a B-24 plane and established an office at the Hotel de Boer.

The Imperial Guard Division sternly guarded the hotel against possible attacks by the Indonesians or by Japanese soldiers not obeying the surrender orders. The Indonesian people in Medan watched this process almost absent-mindedly. In late September, the troop ships of the Allied Forces began entering the ports of Sumatra. The 26th British-Indian Division assigned to Sumatra under the command of Maj. Gen. Chambers, landed at the port of Padang and established its headquarters in Bukit Tinggi, in central Sumatra. In northern Sumatra, one brigade commanded by Brig. Gen. T. E. Kelly landed at Belawan, accompanied by a small Dutch force, and advanced to Medan. They wore long green trousers and short boots. This brigade, composed of British and Indian soldiers, was a force that had recently fought against the Japanese at Akiabu, Burma. The Indians were a mixture of Sikhs from Punjab, Gurkhas from Nepal, and Moslem Tamils. The Dutch force consisted of a small number of Dutch soldiers, native soldiers from Ambon, and others from the Moluccas.

When the Allied Forces advanced to Medan, our Imperial Guard Division transferred the defense of Medan to them and moved the Japanese garrison to the inland estate. Leaving only the liaison office for the Allied Forces in Medan, the Imperial Guard Division headquarters moved to Malihat Estate on the western outskirts of Pematang Siantar, 120 kilometers southeast of Medan. As soon as the Japanese garrison retired, sporadic terrorist attacks against the Allied Forces began in the darkness of a Medan that had been completely quiet until the day before.

On the morning of October 1, the Japanese remaining in Medan were surprised by red and white independence flags which suddenly appeared hanging in all the principal places of Medan. Teuku M. Hasan, who represented Sumatra in the Indonesian Independence Committee, was secretly preparing for independence, keeping in close contact with Sukarno in Java. The previous day he had announced Sumatra's independence to take effect on October 1, with himself as governor.

From this day on, the faces of all the Indonesian people walking in the streets were lively and bright. Until the previous day, they had exchanged greetings, when they saw friends on the street, by saying "*tabek*" (hello). But from now on, they held their right hand up with flushed cheeks, shouting to each other, "*Merdeka!*"

The sign of independence, a small cloth badge of red and white, appeared universally on the breasts of all Indonesians.

On September 30, at midnight, the house of the military government of East Sumatra Province was occupied by those Indonesians forming the newly independent Indonesian government of Sumatra. The Japanese administrators who innocently came to their office the next morning were driven back by Indonesian sentries threatening them with spears. Despite the fact that the Allied Forces were successfully advancing towards Medan, the Indonesians dared to use the office in the center of the city for their government, because the British army commander had declared that there would be no intervention in the domestic affairs of the Dutch East Indies. The peripheral offices in the province that were used by the Japanese military government were also turned into Indonesian government offices.

In addition to the establishment of the independent government, the Indonesian soldiers who had been trained by the Japanese as Giyugun of Heiho, and discharged at the time of the Japanese surrender, quietly gathered back at the Giyugun barracks. They were organized into the public security force, the TKR, with educated youths appointed to various positions as commanders.

The youths who were not absorbed by the TKR were organized into various youth parties, such as Barisan Pemuda Indonesia (BPI) or Pemuda Republic Indonesia (PRI), which became irregular armies collecting various kinds of weapons. There remained, of course, the nationalist party, Partai Nasional Indonesia (PNI), which had existed before the war. The Communists who had been cooperating with the nationalists in resisting the Dutch formed a separate party, Partai Komunis Indonesia (PKI). The educated statesmen organized the Komite Nasional Indonesia (KNI). Many other parties were organized in various places. Most of them were also armed as irregular forces and similarly held high the flag of the independence movement. Collecting weapons such as rifles, pistols, and spears, they began attacking the enemy. It was only a question of time before there would be a great clash against the Allied Forces in Sumatra.

THE SIANTAR INCIDENT

The first clash occurred unexpectedly in an inland city, Pematang Siantar. Siantar was the second largest city of East Sumatra Province -- 500 meters above sea level, 120 kilometers from the capital of Medan, and close to Parapat, the famous resort town by Lake Toba. On October 15, the Dutch army that was settled in barracks in Medan sent a platoon to Siantar. The platoon entered the Siantar Hotel, the best hotel and owned by a Swiss. The hotel had a wide, green, front garden that spread across a road like a public park, and colorful flowers bloomed in profusion on the tropical shrubs.

Initially, the Indonesian people had allowed the Dutch forces to advance freely, directing towards them only their hate-filled eyes. The Dutch officers were in quite high spirits, satisfied by the seemingly craven reaction of the Indonesian people. They raised their glasses of whisky in toasts in the terrace restaurant, and talked arrogantly as they looked down upon the Indonesians watching them from across the garden.

"What? Indonesia proclaiming independence? The Indonesians, who could do nothing if the Japanese had not come, want independence now that the Japanese

Siantar Hotel

have surrendered? They are so foolish as to be ignorant of their own place. Don't be silly. What can such natives do? Once we come and glare at them, they behave like cowards," they boasted, laughing aloud.

The soldiers under the Dutch officers were mostly Ambonese. The Ambonese soldiers were quite proud of their position of belonging to the victorious army. They patrolled the city in small groups, hanging their automatic guns over their shoulders. Many citizens, young and old, male and female, were crowded in the city center where the two-story shop houses, roofed with rust colored tiles, lined the sides of the streets.

The patrolling Ambonese soldiers, ignorant of the fact that they themselves were also natives, were thinking to themselves, "What do you say, foolish natives? Can you say anything to us?!"

They strode around among the people with their shoulders squared. The people gave way to them in fear of their guns, but looked at their backs with disgust. Ambon was one of the islands in the Moluccas, at the eastern end of Indonesian territory. Since the Spanish had conquered this island very early, the inhabitants were the most Europeanized and most were Christians. Consequently, the Dutch used the easily controlled Ambonese as low-class public servants or soldiers and let them confront the Indonesian public. When the Dutch conquered the districts of Indonesia one by one, most soldiers of the conquering forces were Ambonese.

When the patrol came to the front of the crowd in the central market, an innocent Indonesian child called to the Ambonese soldiers because they too were natives, "Merdeka!"

The Ambonese soldiers stopped angrily, saying, "What? What an audacious kid!"

The Ambonese were heretics of the nation called *Belanda Hitam* (Black Dutch), even though they were an Indonesian tribe. Hired by the Dutch as soldiers, they felt it was their highest honor to oppress others of the same race, under the protection of the Dutch forces. They angrily caught the child and slapped its face, pealing off the red and white independence badge. The people exploded in anger.

A fire was thrown on gasoline. A big crowd angrily drew close to the Ambonese soldiers. The atmosphere became dangerous. The astonished Ambonese ran back to the hotel. When the sun was setting, all the youths of the city collected various available weapons and began to attack, encircling the hotel. The Dutch troops resisted with random shooting from automatic guns. Numerous Indonesian youths, however, crawled close on the lawn or through the shrubs and threw fire bottles. The attackers had no organization and moved as individuals, but their numbers were great. In addition, defense was not made easy for the Dutch because the Indonesians were moving as trained by the Japanese. The hotel was finally engulfed by raging flames. The remaining Dutch soldiers shut themselves in an underground cellar, though some escaped out the back. Astute Indonesian youths poured water into the cellar, opening the fire plug, thus suffocating the Dutch there.

After this incident, the Allied Forces could not return to Siantar, and were forced to stay within their base in the Medan-Belawan area. This incident suggested to the Sumatran youths the possibility of defeating the Dutch army armed with modern weapons. Many North Sumatran youths began to gather in Medan to fight with raised spirits.

When this incident occurred, Lt. Col. Muromoto, senior staff officer of the Imperial Guard Division, happened to be in Siantar on his way to his headquarters. He was arrested by the Allied Forces as a war criminal, charged with instigating the Indonesian attack by neglecting to carry out his duty of restoring order, and imprisoned in Medan. Some Dutch spies apparently were in Siantar and informed the Allied Forces. This unexpectedly severe punishment by the Allied Forces was a shock to all Japanese, who intended to maintain their neutrality while being quietly sympathetic toward the Indonesians.

Nevertheless, the incident was a turning point. Afterwards, active youths gathered in Medan from many areas of Sumatra and guerrilla warfare grew steadily. The Allied Forces placed Medan under curfew at night and warned that any person out without permission would be shot. However, guerrilla attacks still occurred every night. Hand grenades were thrown into the Dutch barracks. The British patrol was ambushed. Indian sentries were sniped at from the darkness of the streets.

The Allied Forces called all nationals from Allied countries who were in Sumatra to Medan. They were accommodated in the RAPWI Camp that was located in a European residential area in the center of town and surrounded by two rivers. Allied soldiers encircled the camp. These troops were the main target of the Indonesian night attacks.

TAKE ARMS FROM THE JAPANESE

The war of independence was thus becoming ripe in Sumatra. The Indonesian youths who stood up with literally bare bodies began to seek weapons assiduously. Incidents that occurred in Java informed those in Sumatra. The youths' comrades in Java had already obtained a great number of arms from the Japanese and were fighting the independence war gallantly, becoming a strong military force. The youths in Sumatra naturally began to seek weapons also.

Since the Indonesian youths had many friends in the Japanese army, they visited the Japanese troops to ask their friends for arms. The Japanese, however, were not free to give away weapons because the Allied Forces had strictly prohibited any assistance to the Indonesian independence movement and had ordered the Japanese army to surrender their arms to them before retiring from Sumatra. If weapons were given to the Indonesians, the giver would surely be accused of a war crime. If accused, the accusation would not be restricted to the giver only. How far the accusation would extend was unknown.

In reality, however, a good portion of the arms in Sumatra that had been provided to the volunteer Indonesian soldiers, remained with them, with the excuse that the Japanese had failed to take them back and that they had been inherited by the TKR, the descendent of the volunteer forces.

The national army, the TKR, thus had some arms but it was not the only group demanding weapons. The youth party and most other parties were also fighting guerrilla warfare against the Allied Forces and badly needed arms. Various incidents, such as robbing Japanese soldiers walking alone of their weapons or kidnapping Japanese soldiers along with their arms and automobiles, happened continually. Most troops had some unlisted arms to meet such emergencies, and these steadily flowed to the Indonesians on the periphery, unnoticed by the commanders.

When our Imperial Guard Division had occupied Sumatra, we defended it with the enthusiastic cooperation of the Indonesian people. We firmly believed that the Indonesians were our blood brothers. Our division, therefore, strictly prohibited any firing against Indonesians. All members of the division faithfully and willingly observed this order. Although the Indonesians often raided dumps of military goods, the soldiers on guard only shot into the sky as a warning. As a result, the Indonesians became increasingly bold once they knew the Japanese would fire only warning shots.

Robbing the Japanese of their arms was a patriotic action. The purpose of stealing arms, however, was not simply patriotism. The randomly organized parties of the independence movement competed with each other for power and often competed internally too. They therefore demanded weapons as a means of expanding their parties or winning an internal struggle.

A large-scale arms robbery first occurred in Aceh. The middle-level governing class called Ulebalang and the people's party called PUSA directed by an Islamic teacher were fighting a life-or-death struggle in Aceh. They keenly sought arms to use in the struggle.

The 1st Battalian of the 3rd Imperial Guard Infantry Regiment responsible for middle Aceh, and headquartered in Lhokseumawe, sent a company by train to reinforce the garrison at Bireuen when the struggle between Ulebalang and PUSA escalated. However, the reinforcing company's train was stopped by an obstacle placed on the railway and then surrounded by PUSA youths. The Japanese, who had been prohibited to fire upon Indonesians, could not avoid handing their arms over to the youths. The disarmed company was held hostage to force the garrison at Bireuen to hand over their weapons to the Indonesians.

Another incident occurred in the Sigli area of North Aceh where the struggle between Ulebalang and PUSA was most serious. The two parties were fighting too close to the Japanese garrison of Sigli and endangering it, so the 1st Battalion of the 4th Infantry Regiment staying at Kota Raja sent a platoon in trucks for reinforcement. This platoon was also stopped by the Acehnese at the foot of Mt. Saleh. Captain Maruyama commanded the platoon to surrender all their arms to the Acehnese and sent his subordinates back to Kota Raja. Captain Maruyama then committed suicide by *harakiri*, assuming responsibility for giving arms to the Indonesians against the orders of the Allied Forces.

CHAPTER FOUR
PREVENTION OF A JAPANESE-ACEHNESE BATTLE

To MEDAN ON AN IMPORTANT MISSION

Japanese arms thus began to be transferred to the Acehnese on a large scale. The astonished Allied Forces ordered our Imperial Guard Division to reinforce the Japanese troops in Aceh in restoring order and taking back the arms from the Acehnese. Accordingly, our division headquarters ordered our 4th Infantry Regiment to advance to Aceh. Our regiment, which had been living a hermit's life in Tinjuwan Estate, was no longer able to remain outside history. It was November 23.

Deeply embarrassed, the regimental commander, Col. Kozuma, called me to his office for consultation. The commander was sitting on his rattan chair wearing only his underwear since it was so warm. He explained the situation to me as follows, while repelling the flies with a white priest horsehair swat:

> Capt. Fusayama. I have received an awfully difficult order. What shall we do? If we were to go to Aceh, a fierce battle would surely occur with the Acehnese who are famous for their roughness. As the defeated, we cannot avoid obeying the orders of the Allied Forces. I am seriously embarrassed. Although our Japanese army certainly has the power to defeat the Acehnese, I do not wish to have my soldiers killed or injured in a battle when the war is over. I do not wish to kill the Acehnese either. What do you think? I know you have many close friends among the Indonesians. Could you go to Aceh in advance and negotiate with the Acehnese people, asking them not to resist when we go there, and to return the arms to us without causing trouble?

Listening to him, I was surprised by the gravity of the situation. I thought: Any act of carelessness could lead to a big battle. Although our Japanese army would never lose the battle provided we fought in earnest, our position as the defeated is quite delicate. The Indonesians are now desperate. If mismanaged, hundreds or thousands of lives will be sacrificed on both sides. The sacrifice could even be several tens of thousands if the struggle were to spread to other areas. How absurd it is that we Japanese waste our blood and lives for a battle against the Indonesians who are our brothers! If we were to destroy the Acehnese force, one of the strongest powers in Indonesia, we would with our own hands nip the bud of Indonesian independence which we had bred. We Japanese must by all means prevent such a battle. How can we do it? Although the regiment commander asked me to persuade the Acehnese to return the arms, that will not happen. On the contrary, they will try to get more arms. If we use force against them, a serious battle will surely occur. If such a battle were to occur, the Japanese troops -- disarmed and surrounded in Aceh like hostages -- might be massacred. Although I did not have a particularly confident plan, I answered the commander as follows:

> I understand that you would like to take back the arms from the Acehnese because of the order from the Allied Forces, but that is not possible. The reason I have influence among the Indonesians is because I could never think of taking back the arms but rather would wish from the bottom of my heart to give them more. I am, however, anxious to prevent an armed clash between the Japanese and Indonesians. Let me try to do my best toward that goal. Fortunately, Teuku Moehammadd Hasan, the current governor of Sumatra in independent Indonesia, is my old intimate friend whom I became acquainted with through my study of Acehnese folklore. He himself is an Acehnese who was born in Sigli. Let me go to Medan to consult with Governor Hasan.

The next day, November 24, I left Tinjuwan Estate for Medan. I was accompanied by Lt. Saito, an attaché from the regiment's headquarters, and Lt. Satoh, a former instructor of volunteer Indonesian soldiers, because they were thoughtful and capable officers who spoke the Indonesian language.

AGREEMENT WITH GOVERNOR HASAN

When I arrived at the liaison office of our division in Medan and told of my mission, the members of the office all said: "It will never be possible. We, the defeated Japanese, are now completely despised by the Indonesians. Even the Japanese of high rank such as the divisional staff officers, troop commanders, or senior administrative officers who had been well-acquainted with the Indonesians, were driven back and threatened with spears at the front gate to the Indonesian government compound. Far from negotiation, you will not even be able to enter."

I could guess their meaning. The Japanese they referred to had associated with Indonesians only for matters of official duty, backed by Japanese military power. Once that backing was removed, therefore, it was natural for them to become powerless. My position, however, was different. I had studied folklore, believing that we must understand the life of the inhabitants with whom we were living, without any relation to my official position. There was an Indonesian proverb, *kalau tau, jadi suka* (if you know, you become sympathetic). The leaders of the various Indonesian tribes willingly assisted my folklore study with hearty appreciation and always welcomed me to their homes. I thought, therefore, that Governor Hasan would certainly see me.

Waiting until night, I visited his private residence alone, passing through the darkness of the curfew on a bicycle. His home was in the middle of Bulang Street, east of the central market. It was the familiar house of my old friend. Entering through a gap in a low hedge, I placed my bicycle under the eaves and knocked on the door. Opening the door, Hasan was surprised by my unexpected visit but delightedly admitted me into his drawing room. He was a typical Acehnese with a tall, sturdy brown body. He was a sharp-sighted statesman of complete integrity and a strong will. Hasan had the title of "Meester" because he had studied at a college of law in the Netherlands. He was quite a serious man. In ancient China Confucius said: "The intercourse between *kunshi* (wise men) is plain like water." In this way, we respected and trusted each other, but never exchanged flattering words.

Mr. Teuku Haji Moehammad Hasan in 1945 when he was the first Governor of Sumatra inindependent Indonesia

Hasan was already in his sarong to relax for the evening, but he opened his eyes wide in apprehension when he heard my direct explanation. When I finished he looked straight into my eyes, saying:

If the Japanese army sends additional troops to Aceh, a battle is unavoidable. Since you have studied Acehnese folklore, I think you know the history of the Acehnese War, in which the Dutch were embarrassed by the difficulty they had in achieving victory, taking as long as thirty years. It is preposterous to try to suppress such self-respecting people by military force. I do not like either to kill Japanese soldiers or to have our important Acehnese force destroyed by the Japanese army. Why do you wish to reinforce your troops in Aceh? The actual wish of the Japanese army is, I believe, to repatriate to Japan as soon as possible. You, therefore, had better withdraw from Aceh to prepare for repatriation.

Incidentally, I am seeing Lt. General Christison, commander of the Allied Forces in the Dutch East Indies, who is flying from Java to Medan the day after tomorrow. I will vigorously protest this to him. From your side, too, please do your best to stop the reinforcements and withdraw as soon as possible. If you withdraw all Japanese troops in Aceh, I will go there to persuade the Acehnese people to secure the life and property of the withdrawing Japanese. This will be possible because I myself am Acehnese.

Although this proposal was quite different from the directive that I had been given by the regiment commander, it seemed to me to be the best plan. There was no other means by which to prevent the battle between the Acehnese and the Japanese. I approved wholeheartedly of his proposal. We then agreed to meet at the Indonesian government offices the next day to make the agreement formal in the presence of the relevant people. When I described the interim agreement to the members of the liaison office on my return, all of them said with an air of disbelief: "This would be the best thing if it is really possible. But it does not seem possible to change the orders of the almighty victor to whom we have surrendered unconditionally."

The next day, October 25, I went to the Indonesian government offices, accompanied by Lt. Saito and Lt. Satoh. The Indonesian sentries presented arms and politely admitted us into the office. From the Indonesian side, Maharaja Soankupon Siregar, the assistant governor, and Tengku Hafas, the East Sumatra provincial resident, attended with Governor Teuku Moehammad Hasan. Although the two had been former acquaintances of mine, they sat in a dignified and strained manner. We thus made formal the interim agreement of the previous night.

A DESPERATE ENTREATY

On returning to the liaison office, I immediately reported this agreement to the divisional chief staff officer, Col. Okada, who happened to be staying there, and asked him to support me in negotiating with the Allied Forces. Listening to my detailed explanation, he understood that the agreement was the best possible solution and agreed to go with me to the British brigade headquarters to see the commander. Such an action by the divisional chief staff officer in responding to a proposal of a young enlisted officer who was not on the staff of the division headquarters, was unthinkable prior to the end of the war. However, he unexpectedly accepted my proposal and immediately put it into action because after the war, our division was very willing to listen to the opinions of anyone, regardless of rank, in order to find the best solutions and use the most able men to resolve difficulties.

At the British brigade headquarters, with the support of the silent Col. Okada, I explained to the commander, Brig. Gen. Kelly, the history of the Acehnese people tenaciously resisting Dutch force for thirty years in the Acehnese War and that they were also fanatic believers in Islam who were not afraid of dying in a Holy War. I further entreated him as follows:

> Consequently, if our Japanese army were to advance to Aceh for reinforcement, it will surely cause an all-out war. I do not think it is your intention to order the Japanese to open war again after the Pacific War is over. I cannot imagine you would want to use us in the war against the Indonesians (the use of a defeated force for military purposes was prohibited by an international law agreed upon in The Hague). However, your order to advance to Aceh is essentially an order to make war. Please do not let us make war again. Instead, please give an order to withdraw, as soon as possible, all Japanese

troops remaining in Aceh. Your Excellency, Brig. Gen. Kelly, please ask your headquarters in Java to order the withdrawal of our troops from Aceh.

The person in front of me was the victor, the enemy against whom we had fought. I wondered if he would really appreciate our difficulties. I was nervously afraid that he would maliciously and mercilessly reject my entreaty. I had fearfully entreated him, even though I felt I was risking my own life. To my surprise, Brig. Kelly listened to me with a polite earnestness and answered me frankly, "I understand your situation. I will do my best to solve the problem in consultation with my superiors."

I could hardly believe that this person was actually one of the British whom we Japanese had thus far despised, saying "brutal English and Americans," and who had established the vicious colonialism that had ruled the seven seas without regarding non-Europeans as human.

The next day, Lt. Gen. Christison, commander of the whole Allied Forces in the Dutch East Indies, flew to Medan. As scheduled, he met with Brig. Kelly and the Indonesian governor, Hasan. In accordance with his agreement with me, Hasan protested sternly to Gen. Christison:

> In Singapore, before coming to Indonesia, you declared that you were coming to Indonesia only to disarm and repatriate the Japanese forces and had no intention of intervening in the domestic affairs of Indonesia. If you order the Japanese army to reinforce the troops in Aceh, a battle will surely result. The order, therefore, means that your British army will attack our independence forces, using the Japanese army. It obviously contradicts your declaration. You should immediately prevent such an unjust plan. If you want to avoid trouble, you should withdraw all Japanese troops from Aceh.

Hasan informed me by telephone that Christison said he understood, but I was not yet free from anxiety. The problem was the Dutch army which had come together with the British. The Dutch were the ones who most wished to have the Japanese army destroy the Indonesian independence forces. I could not yet feel free from danger. I was still afraid that this negotiation I rested my life on might be reversed by some maneuver.

Do YOUR BEST AND LEAVE THE REST TO GOD

The honest and gentle attitude of the British brigade commander towards us made me feel some hope. However, I was afraid that some foolish Japanese troops might rashly advance to Aceh and cause useless confusion before they were informed of a definite change in orders by the Allied Forces. Consequently, I hurriedly returned to Tinjuwan Estate and told my regiment commander: "Please postpone the departure to Aceh, taking as much time for preparation as possible because I hope the order to advance to Aceh will be withdrawn. Please continue with preparations only."

The regiment commander looked disbelieving at the possibility. He said, "Well, I wonder if the Allied Forces will accede so easily to our request since the British and the Dutch are conspirators. Our division commander, too, may not be bold enough to postpone for long executing the order of the Allied Forces."

In reality, however, day by day he delayed, ordering preparations for the march to continue without actually marching, because he himself was also not really willing to march to Aceh.

To improve our chances, I also visited the commander of the 5th Imperial Guard Infantry Regiment, Maj. Gen. Sawamura, who remained in the district of Tebing Tinggi, to explain the situation and ask him to advise the division commander to change the advance order. I had deep respect for the personality of Gen. Sawamura in the past and relied upon him. Thereafter, I visited the commanders of the 3rd Infantry and other regiments, one after another, and asked them to support the withdrawal at the commanders' meeting of the division. The 3rd Regiment commander, of course, agreed with my opinion because it was his troops who had stayed in Bireuen and Lhokseumawe as the disarmed hostages. All the other commanders also listened to me, nodding earnestly. I therefore became increasingly confident. Several days passed without any orders arriving from the division headquarters either to stop preparations for the march or to urge the march on.

I had done everything possible that I could think of. The rest could only be left to God. Anyhow, we should never advance to Aceh. On returning to Tinjuwan Estate, I began to farm again with my company, as if I was perfectly confident of the change in orders. All the other companies of the regiment who were still engaged in preparing for the advance watched my company curiously.

My soldiers had no doubts at all. As soon as breakfast was over, all members, including myself, went out to the farm. When the fallen, decayed oil palm trees were removed, a poisonous snake, a cobra, crept out from under the trunk. On finding the cobra, the soldiers beat the snake to death with a shout of joy and then continued to cultivate the land. A road was made through the center of our farm and rows of papaya trees were planted on both sides to improve our self-sufficiency. The oil-palm woods spreading beyond our farm became greener and the red earth of the farm we cultivated day by day also became green, under the grace of the tropical sunshine.

During this period, the Japanese troops in Aceh, who had been disarmed and surrounded by the Acehnese, were suffering from an increased sense of isolation and trembled with powerlessness, observing the internal struggle of the Acehnese. PUSA, the people led by the religious teachers, and the Ulebalang, the ruling middle class, were fighting a life and death struggle. Particularly in the areas of Sigli and Bireuen, they were continuing a serious struggle of murder and trickery.

CHAPTER FIVE
TO RIOTS IN MEDAN

APPOINTED AS LIAISON OFFICER IN MEDAN

One day after spending about a week this way, my regiment commander suddenly sent an orderly for me. He told me that I had been appointed by our division to the position of liaison officer managing Indonesian affairs at the liaison office in Medan. My regiment commander, Col. Kozuma, said gloomily:

> The current situation is so difficult everywhere. If you go to Medan, I will deeply miss a reliable consultant. However, the divisional chief staff officer, Col. Okada, has eagerly asked me to lend you for a while to the liaison office in Medan because you are the only Japanese who can talk with the senior Indonesian leaders in the present situation. The division commander, Lt. Gen. Kunomura, also requested this. I therefore could not help granting the request. You must go, but please come back as soon as the situation is resolved.

Kozuma watched me helplessly.

In reality, our regiment also had a number of problems. Since the war ended, the control of rank-and-file soldiers had become quite difficult. Even within the regiment headquarters, officers and soldiers when drinking would take up their swords and cry, "I will go and kill the regiment commander!" It was said that the reason the commander had inserted my company barracks between his residence and the barracks of the regiment's soldiers was to protect him with my well-disciplined soldiers. In a defeated army there were also a number of other problems that were difficult to solve with the knowledge learnt at a military academy.

On the other hand, I was not a little embarrassed by suddenly receiving such an order. The detailed situation in Medan immediately before and after the end of the war was completely unknown to me. Because I had stayed in Medan both as a wireless platoon commander and as a headquarters attache of the divisional communications troops, I knew every corner of that city well at that time. I had moved, however, to Aceh one month before the war's end, being appointed as the communication company commander of the 4th Infantry Regiment. So I knew nothing about the changes in Medan before and after the Japanese surrender. After the war's end, I had merely passed through Medan and was settled in Tinjuwan Estate, far inland in East Sumatra Province, buried in seclusion. I was seriously embarrassed by this sudden appointment to a very important office that was responsible for the management of an extremely complicated political crisis, after spending the rapidly changing postwar period living a hermit's life, farming when clear, and reading when rainy, completely isolated for three months from the outside world.

However, I had also personally observed just a week previously the fact that the relationship between the Indonesians and the Medan liaison office had foundered, even though it was functioning well with the Allied Forces. Since the members of the office had marvelled at the success of the agreement I made with Governor Hasan by personally visiting his home, it seemed naturally to lead to this result. I could not help making up my mind to do my best. Leaving the affairs of my company to Lt. Kamiya, my senior officer, I left Tinjuwan Estate in a truck, accompanied by a driver and an orderly. Before going to Medan, I went to the divisional headquarters in Malihat Estate.

Malihat Estate was a tea farm situated in the rolling hills. The divisional headquarters was in the center, shaded by huge, dark green, tropical trees. A six angle, glass-windowed section of the house was the staff office. I first checked the papers on the desk of the office to find out the general situation, and found a telegram from the 25th Army Headquarters addressed to Lt. Gen. Kunomura, Imperial Guard Division commander. In the telegram, the army commander ordered our divisional commander to prepare for the withdrawal of the troops in Aceh, informing him that the Allied Forces commander in Java had withdrawn the order to reinforce the Japanese army in Aceh and permitted their withdrawal. I could finally confirm my success. The agreement with Governor Hasan, that I had made, had borne fruit. An unfortunate Japanese-Acehnese clash had been prevented. My small effort had saved thousands or even tens of thousands of people from useless death or injury. I felt an unspeakable satisfaction and a swelling of self-confidence.

I greeted the divisional commander and received relevant instructions from the chief staff officer and others. Once again I climbed in the truck and headed for Medan. I sat beside the driver, and my orderly stood on the loading platform looking ahead over the roof of the driving cabin.

ANGER AGAINST THE SENTRIES POINTING THEIR SPEARS

My truck left Malihat Estate and, via the city of Pematang Siantar, drove down the asphalt road, passing through continuous rubber estates. Driving 40 kilometers to the north, we reached the city of Tebing Tinggi. When I had passed through here a week previously, this city was guarded by the 5th Infantry Regiment, but this time, I found no Japanese sentries either at the entrance or within the city. Without paying much attention, we passed through a corner of the city and came onto the road for Medan, crossing the 70 meter long bridge over the Padang River. We were surprised to find an unexpected barricade, entwined with barbed wire, blocking the road.

I stopped our truck, wondering what was the matter, and approached the barricade. Four Indonesian youths who had been sitting in a hut built under a stand of coconut trees on the side of the road, suddenly rushed towards me. In a line they blocked me and simultaneously pointed their spears at my chest. They had long spears with red tassels that had been provided them by the Japanese army when they were Heiho before the end of the war. The Japanese army gave rifles to the Giyugun but spears to the Heiho because no more surplus rifles were available.

I had trained the Heiho and taught them the use of this spear. I was a man who was believed, both by myself and others, to be the best friend of the Indonesian people, having many close friends among Indonesian leaders. Nevertheless, the Indonesian youths whom I believed to be on my side, had dared direct their spears at me. An uncontrollable anger exploded in my heart. Stepping toward the spear tips, I shouted "Who are you? The Japanese and Indonesians are brothers. We Japanese are your brothers. Why do you direct your spears at me? For what purpose is this barricade? Why do you stop us? Open it! Open it immediately!"

I again stepped forward, shouting angrily. I had a pistol at my waist, but I did not touch it. The youths directing their spears at me, however, stepped back, overwhelmed by my anger. The astonished chief guard who had remained in the hut came up in a hurry with a rifle saying, "Just a moment, Sir. Don't be so angry. I will open the barricade."

He hastily opened the barricade, assisted by the youths. Without changing my expression, I ordered my driver to pass through. The whole incident had lasted only a few minutes.

A STRANGE ATMOSPHERE

As I recalled the incident a short time later, while calming down from the excitement as we drove on, I felt a chill up my spine. It seemed very strange. The atmosphere was really funny. Something very dangerous could happen if we weren't careful.

Sensing a threatening situation in the bottom of my heart without knowing why, I ordered my driver to go at full speed. We hurried straight for Medan, stirring the palm leaves on the road side with gusts of wind. I was later informed in Medan that the Japanese estate managers in the area were all captured by Indonesian youths and killed one by one. Just on that day, the youths of the Tebing area took, by extortion, from the Japanese army their right to guard the city. They were planning to attack small groups of Japanese troops, killing them one by one to take their weapons. If I had carelessly permitted the sentries to stop us back there, our lives would surely have been lost. Although at the time I did not know of the situation, the weird atmosphere had alerted my sixth sense to the serious danger.

Looking askance through the window of the moving truck at the many Indonesian sentries standing with spears, I was deeply afflicted, thinking of my work in Medan. "The atmosphere is very strange. What are the current political conditions in Indonesia? The atmosphere seems completely different from a week ago when we last visited Medan. At the Medan liaison office, I must solve the various problems in negotiation with the Indonesian government, but I know nothing about the internal conditions of the Indonesian society behind the government. How can I carry on my diplomatic negotiations in a proper way without knowing the background conditions?"

However, how lucky I was! It happened that a clue for understanding the background to the riot was waiting on my arrival in Medan.

CHAPTER SIX
THE FIFTH CORPS OF THE YOUTH PARTY

FREEDOM FIGHTER OR AGENT OF NICA?

At that time, the situation in East Sumatra Province around Medan was far more entangled than that in Acehnese Province. As mentioned earlier, the Dutch forces had founded a special agency named the Netherlands Indies Civil Administration (NICA) in order to reestablish colonial government in the former Dutch territory and destroy the Indonesian independence movement.

NICA was working on the pro-Dutch Indonesians, using a large amount of political funds. There were actually a number of people who wished to revive the dream of prosperity under patronage of the Dutch government that they had looked forward to before the Japanese advance. They were mostly Indonesians of the local governing class, the past senior bureaucrats, and the Chinese and other non-Indonesian Asians. NICA endeavored to get them on the Dutch side. Lt. Col. Knottenbelt was reportedly the chief of NICA in Sumatra. He was an excellent strategist and very useful to the Netherlands. In the beginning, NICA tried to get the pro-Dutch Indonesians to sign a list of cooperators, but later they had to move underground because their open approach had caused a serious reaction from the independence parties. NICA sought not only conspirators among the native inhabitants, but also infiltrated into various Indonesian classes Indonesian spies who had been captured on the coast during the war and educated at a spy school in Australia. They were used to secretly disturb the thoughts of the Indonesian people. Meanwhile, Lt. Col. Knottenbelt concealed even his own whereabouts.

As a result, it became very difficult to distinguish between the independence supporters and the secret conspirators, particularly in the

Medan area because it was inhabited by a mixture of races. With mingling suspicion and struggles for power, internal strife was repeated throughout the various fighting groups. During this strife, the call of *kaki tangan Nika* appeared as a fatal definition for a person. In the Indonesian language, *kaki* meant leg and *tangan* meant hand. *Kaki tangan* meant an Indonesian traitor working as a tool of the Dutch secret agency. Once a person was defined as tool of NICA, he could not escape being ruined by the hostility of the Indonesian people.

Burglars began to break into houses in Medan. The burglar would pose as a patriotic thief and declare, "You are the tool of NICA. You must be punished. We are confiscating all your property for the independence war fund." By so declaring, robbery became justice. The burglar took as much property as possible, including furniture, such as doors, and electric appliances, and carried them away openly in trucks. It was said that the victims should appreciate that they were not robbed of their lives. On the walls along the streets, the slogan, "*Hancurkan NIKA* [crush NICA]," was painted in huge letters. In accordance with this slogan, tools of NICA were repeatedly attacked every day somewhere in Medan.

Although the independence movement itself looked brilliant, too many parties randomly raised their flags in competition with each other. Deserters from the Japanese army were secretly assisting them in many places. The spies of NICA were believed to be penetrating even the independence parties. Differentiation between the real freedom fighters and NICA was thus very difficult.

THE YOUTH PARTY AND THE FIFTH CORPS

Initially the youths who were not absorbed by the TKR (Tentera Keamanan Rakyat or People's Security Force) organized the PRI (Pemuda Republik Indonesia or the Indonesian Republic Youth Party). The name was, however, altered to Pesindo (Pemuda Sosialis Indonesia or the Socialist Indonesian Youth Party) in Java in November 1945. This reorganization was reportedly directed by the underground Communists, such as Amir Sjarifuddin, Sudisman, and others, who favored a Communist revolution linked to Moscow, and disliked the nationalistic liberation movement being at the initiative of the elderly political leaders and past volunteer soldiers sympathetic to the Japanese. The radical youths agitated by the demagoguery spread by the Communists, killed many Japanese and finally invited a counterattack by the Japanese army in Central Java. The character of the youth party had thus, in this way, changed.

On the periphery such as Sumatra, however, the shift to Pesindo was in name only and the party was still composed of the same nationalistic youths. Since the leaders in Java initially hid the fact that they were Communists, the youths on the periphery danced innocently, believing they were simply supporting independence. Pesindo expanded rapidly, absorbing the youths who were not organized by the TKR and in the process became much bigger than the TKR. Pesindo took the initiative in the independence movement everywhere, ignoring the Indonesian government and the TKR.

In contrast to the TKR, Pesindo received no financial support from the government. Consequently, it was obliged to support itself by collecting a private tax directly from the people, particularly wealthy Chinese merchants. Since the tax was collected by force with no regulation, such a tax was often difficult to differentiate from robbery. The Indonesian government was seriously embarrassed by such theft, but Pesindo could not be ignored as it was a strong force for independence. Within Pesindo, Pasukan Kelima (the Fifth Corps) was believed to be the most active participant in such outrageous activities, though its parent party, Pesindo, was also moving in a similar way.

Pasukan Kelima was a special branch composed of only the Bataks. Although Pesindo did not have any Third or Fourth Corps, it was named the Fifth Corps after the model of the 5th Column of Franco's force in the Spanish Civil War. Franco said that "though our force is marching in four columns, we have a fifth column that is harassing the enemy's rear position and secretly penetrating." Pasukan Kelima moved, however, not underground like the Spanish 5th Column, but openly as an unabashed force for the independence movement.

Commanding the Fifth Corps was a Toba Batak, Sihite, who was born in the town of Tarutung in the center of the Tapanuli Highlands. Before the war's end, he was a contractor of engineering work and a part-time broker of various goods. He was an unusually shrewd man and cleverly cooperated with the Japanese army, obtaining contracts for the construction of most military airfields in northern Sumatra. However, while cooperating in this way, he was once imprisoned for stealing a large number of goods from the Japanese army and selling them to the Japanese navy. Because of his shrewdness, his activity in the black market was more remarkable than any other person's, even after the war's end. After founding the Fifth Corps by gathering people from his tribe, he boldly earned still more money through the black market, under protection of the independence movement. He was thus able to establish great power, getting weapons faster than many other parties. It was not very clear from where he got the weapons.

This corps had a broad organization, with branches in most principal towns. They were believed to be freedom fighters as well as robbers. They were rumored to steal arms and goods not only from the Japanese army but also from the Allied Forces -- sometimes even from the stores of the independent Indonesian government. The robbers were not only Pesindo and Pasukan Kelima. Various groups robbed the wealthy houses in Medan one after another. But the Fifth Corps was believed to be the most active in such thefts. Initially, only the Chinese merchants favored by the Allied Forces were targeted as traitors. Later, however, the robbery was directed against all wealthy Chinese regardless of evidence of betrayal. It was also directed against Indian merchants, and finally even against Indonesian merchants. The police could take no action against them.

The Indonesian national army, TKR, composed of past volunteer soldiers trained by the Japanese army, had the most order and discipline. The independence government eventually ordered the military police from the TKR to capture Sihite, but he was soon released because the Fifth Corps threatened the military police with mass-encirclement. Neither the civil police nor the military police could touch the Fifth Corps. The Chinese organized a band of vigilantes but they merely invited even fiercer attack, since the Allied Forces were not intended to guard the Chinese. The wealthy Chinese merchants were finally compelled to ask the Fifth Corps to protect them by paying them money.

Although those youth bands were fighting for the independence movement, they ignored the independence government and walked around with shoulders squared, claiming that they were leading the struggle. They formed their own police units. They also created a suicide fighters' unit, dressed in black uniforms, in imitation of the Japanese or German suicide attack units. The Fifth Corps, or Pasukan Kelima, was eventually no longer considered a branch of Pesindo. It became a separate party in competition with its former parent.

The power of the Fifth Corps grew day by day. Its former parent party, Pesindo, and the Communist and nationalist parties also created their own armed forces. The Indonesian independence government and the national army, which had initially led the independence movement, were now being left behind by the various irregular forces. The independence movement was thus thrown into utter confusion. The freedom fights and internal fights were helplessly intermingled in the city of Medan. It was under such conditions that I arrived at my new post.

I FIND MY FRIENDS IN THE FIFTH CORPS

The Medan liaison office was on Lombok Avenue, one of several avenues branching to the south from Serdang Street which ran from west to east in the northern part of Medan. There were footpaths on both sides of the avenue, though it was not very wide. Some ten Western-style single-story houses with small lawns and gardens lined both sides, and the liaison office made use of the majority of these houses, placing sentry guards at both ends of the avenue. The guards permitted the public to pass freely during the day, since citizens lived in the other houses, but a pass was necessary to come through at night.

On my arrival at the liaison office, I found several Indonesian youths setting furniture down from a truck parked just in front of my truck. One of them suddenly approached me, opening his arms and crying, "Oh my! Tuan [Mr.] Fusayama. I've missed you for a long time. Where were you and what have you been doing since I last saw you?"

Liaison office at Lombok Avenue

Fifth Corps office at Lombok Avenue

"Oh, Ismed. After we lost the war, I thought I would never see you again. From Aceh, where I stayed until the war's end, I moved to Tinjuwan Estate, where until yesterday I was farming," I replied. Ismed was an intelligent Batak youth with whom I had kept close company when I was in Medan. He showed unchanged affection for me, even though I was an officer of the miserably defeated Japanese army. I held his hand firmly, filled with deep emotion.

He briefly told me his story. When the war was over, he returned to his father's home in Pematang Siantar because he was laid off by the Mitsui Bussan Company for which he was working. In the middle of October, Dutch troops advanced to the city and caused the Siantar incident that I described earlier. Together with his comrades, he gallantly attacked the Dutch troops who had run into the Siantar Hotel and defeated them. At that time, hearing that two Ambonese soldiers had escaped by jeep, he hurried in his father's car to pursue the jeep, accompanied by two of his comrades, and they arrived in Medan. Staying on in Medan, he joined the intelligence unit of the Fifth Corps after finding that his cousin, Nirwan, was chief, and that several others who had been his friends when he lived in Medan previously were members.

The intelligence unit was organized by Nirwan, vice-commander of the Fifth Corps, along with the bright young men who were close to him. Like the staff office of an army division, this group was responsible for collecting information and planning guerrilla operations. Since the headquarters of the corps had too many people moving in and out, they looked for a quieter place and found a vacant house on a corner of Lombok Avenue adjacent to the Japanese liaison office. When I met him, they were just moving furniture into the house. It was really a curious coincidence. Quite unexpectedly, I got my first contact with the Fifth Corps -- the clue to the chaos -- no sooner than taking my first step in my new post in Medan.

The Fifth Corps' coming to live on this same avenue, however, gave no little uneasiness to my comrades in the liaison office. They said to me, "Some very unwelcome people have come in to live. It means that we have robbers almost in our house. Please be very careful."

The intelligence unit of the Fifth Corps was, however, a golden opportunity for me. Diplomatic action without knowing the hidden background in such a time of chaos is like the house cleaning of a blind person. While appreciating the kind warning from my comrades, I willingly made advances toward the group.

THE YOUTHS OF THE INTELLIGENCE UNIT

Because their house was on Lombok Avenue and thus guarded by the soldiers of our liaison office, the intelligence unit asked me for passes to get by the sentries. With pleasure I offered them the passes but did not forget to examine their backgrounds, since the passes could only be given after a background check. The twelve youths in the unit were all graduates from high school or college, and included two medical doctors. They explained themselves as follows:

> It is true that a number of rascals can be found in the Fifth Corps. However, the members of our intelligence unit are all sons of good families. We shall never trouble you. Our unit is under the direct control of our commander and is responsible for analyzing information and planning guerrilla activities. We chose this house for our office because our activities are difficult to carry out from inside the headquarters.

The head of the unit, Nirwan, was the second son of Maharaja Soankupon Siregar, the assistant governor. Nirwan was the most intimate with me among the sons of Soankupon. When I first met him, he was a clerk at the Medan Higher Court. He was the brightest of Soankupon's sons and always had a clear opinion on various problems. He particularly enjoyed engaging in frank and free criticism of the Japanese military administration to me, a Japanese officer, since I always listened to him smiling. When Sihite organized the corps, collecting together the youths of his race, Nirwan was invited to assume the position of second vice-commander. He then organized this intelligence unit, gathering his close friends, to act as the brains of Sihite, who was not very educated.

Ismed, whom I had first met on Lombok Avenue, was one of Nirwan's cousins and so he also belonged to a Batak royal family from Sipirok. He was the first son of a millionaire who owned a large rubber estate in Pematang Siantar. Prevented from studying abroad by the war, Ismed worked for a Japanese business firm. Since he was the son of a millionaire, never lacking in pocket money, and had a cheerful personality, he had many male and female friends in Medan. I met him often at the house of Mr. Pulungan, close to my barracks, where he once lodged. Ismed was quite a sociable person, knowing a lot of the gossip in detail, and he talked cheerfully at the tea table. It was great fun for me to hear his small talk, while sinking deep in a rattan armchair on the terrace of Pulungan's house, under the light of the beautiful moon.

When a Japanese girl came to work at his company, he adored her so much that he almost forgot himself, saying to me, "The Japanese girl smells heavenly." His adoration sounded so odd that Mr. Pulungan's elder daughter glared at him. I had so many pleasant memories of him like that. Ismed, whom I remembered as such an innocent, cheerful youth, was now a political fighter for freedom, displaying a pistol hung at his waist. When his comrades shouted to him, "Merdeka!" he responded holding up his right hand gallantly, "*Seratos Prosen* (100%)!" I could not help but look at him with wide eyes, surprised by the remarkable change in him.

Two unique members of the Fifth Corps were the two sons of the first vice commander of the corps, Dr. Nainggolan. The elder son, Bob, was a physician who worked for the Indonesian volunteer army until the end of the war. The younger son, Boyke, also entered the volunteer army and was promoted to the position of second lieutenant. He was an extremely hot-blooded man.

Pane was the only non-Batak member. He had a broad-shouldered, sturdy physique, and was respected for his extraordinarily strong, mental and physical powers. Jusuf was a quite different type of youth, having pale skin and a slim and handsome body. He was a pure and sensitive-hearted romantic. Though I have not mentioned them all, a variety of wonderful youths were in the unit. All of them were absorbed in the independence movement with the innocence of children.

THE BAD REPUTATION OF SIHITE

However, the Fifth Corps commander, Sihite, had a very bad reputation. I often heard the following rumors from my comrades:

> The Fifth Corps is very suspicious. It would be a fatal mistake if you were to think that the Fifth Corps is party of the independence movement. It is said that Sihite is a secret agent receiving a million

guilders from the Dutch forces through a Czech named Schmitt.

You see? The Fifth Corps has the greatest number of arms such as pistols. It is said that they were given to the corps by the Dutch. The aim of the Dutch is presumably to have the reinforced Fifth Corps attack the British and Japanese in order to make them angry, and then destroy the power of the Indonesian independence movement. This is a very clever strategy of NICA, aiming to pound Indonesians by using other powers and, at the same time, to transform the Indonesian grudge against the Dutch to the Japanese. The head of NICA, Col. Knottenbelt, is a very clever man.

It is said that Sihite is receiving a salary of ten thousand guilders per month. Sihite is keeping this relationship completely secret, without telling even his own staff. In ignorance of the truth, believing that they are fighting for independence, his followers are actually dancing to destroy their own independence. Sihite is carrying a special pass in the bottom of his shoes to pass through the sentry line of the Allied Forces. He shows the pass to the Allied Forces' sentry by taking off his shoes, they say.

It was not known to what extent these rumors were true. A number of suspicious signs were, nevertheless, found around him. Most of the people at the liaison office believed that Sihite had secret contacts with Col. Knottenbelt who was a well-known expert in plotting. There was no way for me to confirm this because, after surrendering, we no longer had an intelligence network. The many suspicious signs, however, were difficult to deny. It seemed true that Sihite owned a hidden house inside the RAPWI Camp, guarded by the Allied Forces, because his figure was occasionally seen by Japanese liaison officers visiting the Allied Forces office within the camp. Although there was no definite proof that Sihite was a traitor, my comrades in the liaison office kindly and repeatedly warned me in all seriousness: "We believe that Sihite is a traitor. If you speak carelessly to the members of the Fifth Corps, believing them to be independence fighters, it might cause dreadful trouble for you. Please do not be careless when talking with them because everything will be directly heard by NICA."

However, whether or not Sihite was a traitor, I could not doubt the pure passion for independence displayed by the youths of the intelligence unit who were my old friends. As they held hands and cried, "Merdeka!" and replied, "Seratos Prosen!" their eyes burned with passion for independence and showed no moral turpitude. I sometimes tried to mention Sihite's reputation to them, but they never took any notice and praised him instead as the most capable hero of the independence movement, relying on him with absolute confidence. They answered, "It is merely the counter-propaganda of the counterforce."

CHAPTER SEVEN
A STRATEGY OF ANTI-JAPANESE AGITATION

AT THE HOUSE OF RESIDENT HAFAS

The day after my arrival at the liaison office in Medan, I visited the governor of Sumatra, Teuku Moehammad Hasan, at his office to inform him that our Japanese army had begun to prepare for the withdrawal of their troops from Aceh, with permission of the Allied Forces. Governor Hasan flew delightedly to Kota Raja in a Japanese airplane and began to travel by car from the north through the province, persuading the Acehnese people to allow the Japanese troops to withdraw peacefully. Capt. Adachi, a former commander of the Japanese special agency in Aceh, who had enjoyed the confidence of the Acehnese in PUSA, accompanied Hasan to ensure cooperation from the Japanese side. One by one they visited the towns where the Japanese troops were, persuading the Acehnese to protect the lives and property of the withdrawing Japanese. Their journey was not easy because they were jostled by the internal struggle between PUSA and the Ulebalang, and their lives were often endangered. While they were carrying out their desperate effort in Aceh, the atmosphere in East Sumatra province rapidly turned worse in the absence of Governor Hasan.

The day after Hasan's departure, I visited the private residence of the Resident of East Sumatra Province, Tengku Hafas, for negotiations over the temporary lodging of the Japanese estate managers who were retiring from various estates. Tengku Hafas was talking with a visitor when I arrived at his house.

Hafas was an aristocrat from a distinguished family related to the Sultan of Deli and Raja Bedagai. He was also a famous millionaire. His house was an elegant European-style building with a wide lawn and a terrace located on the east side of Raja Street, which ran south from the center of Medan. The whole house was decorated with incredibly beautiful furniture. I noticed a young girl in a typical Malay dress cross the inner corridor. She was extremely beautiful with a polite demeanor. Her father, Hafas, was also a handsome gentleman, though his face was a little long and his Charlie Chaplin-like mustache was not to my taste. With a slender chained and gilt-edged eye-glass resting on his aristocratic nose, he was talking with the visitor in a low voice, his eyes blinking awkwardly under the glass. The visitor was a short and slim, dark-colored man, with sharp eyes. Placing a black briefcase on a low coffee table, he was discussing something with Hafas in a low but fierce tone, looking sharply into the eyes of Hafas.

I waited in the next room and watched the conversation in the main drawing room through the wide open door. Since the conversation seemed to continue for a long time, I interrupted to announce the purpose of my visit. Tengku Hafas, whom I had believed to be a gentle and timid man, turned with an unexpectedly sharp attitude and gave me a brusque reply while glancing at the eyes of the visitor. I almost became angry, wondering why, when we had been acquainted from before, he assumed such an attitude. I barely managed to calm myself, thinking, "His response is curious. There must be some reason. He looks afraid of the visitor. Who is this visitor?"

So I withdrew, returning to the sofa, and continued to listen casually to the conversation, eating the rice crackers served in a bowl. Although I could not understand the low-voiced, quick-spoken Indonesian, I noticed a red and white independence badge signed PSI-PV on the visitor's chest when he stood up after finishing the conversation. PSI was the mark of Pesindo and PV was the mark of Pasukan Kelima or the Fifth Corps. Though it was the first time I'd seen him, my sixth sense suggested to me that he might be the first vice-commander of the Fifth Corps, Dr. Nainggolan. He went out by the porch, giving me a short and sharp glance, and got into his car. On the back of his car, driven by dark-colored man typical of the Toba Batak, I observed a plate marked "PV."

RADICALS THREATEN GOVERNMENT LEADERS

After seeing his visitor off at the porch, Tengku Hafas changed his attitude towards me as if he had become completely different person. He began to apologize in a very polite and sociable manner, "Please pardon me, I really apologize. Please do not be displeased. It was...."

I said, laughing lightly, "Please do not worry. I understand. You were concerned about your visitor's feelings."

Hafas recovered his bright smile. He talked rapidly, after carefully looking around: "Oh, you do understand. I really do apologize. These days, it is fatal to be labeled by such radicals as the agent of NICA or pro-Dutch. An intimate relationship with the Japanese must also be hidden these days. I know my attitude towards you was very impolite. But please be patient. If I were stamped by them as a weak-kneed diplomat or a person acting for profit on behalf of the enemy, who knows what would happen to me? If I was murdered as a traitor, what would happen to my beloved daughter and family? I hardly know how to excuse myself to you. But please pretend to be on bad terms with me in front of such people. When I suddenly show you such a rough attitude, please act as if you were in a quarrel with me. It is a really difficult time. I am very sorry. Please understand and help me."

Recalling the man who had threatened Hafas a few minutes ago by sharply looking into his eyes, I felt again that he might be Nainggolan, the vice-commander of Pasukan Kelima. So I asked Hafas, "That man was Dr. Nainggolan, wasn't he?"

I had hit the mark. According to Hafas, Nainggolan was better educated and cleverer than the commander, Sihite. Actually, Sihite was the boss of thugs. Hafas had to be more careful with Dr. Nainggolan, since he was much sharper. He was the father of Bob and Boyke of the intelligence unit, whom I was seeing every day. In contrast to the quite open-hearted appearance of his sons, he conveyed a strangely dark and cold impression. And the darkness of the vice-commander seemed to represent the darkness of the Fifth Corps.

NEWSPAPERS TURN ANTI-JAPANESE

Just at this time, the press comments suddenly turned anti-Japanese, proving that Hafas' words were true.

The Japanese are not friends of the Indonesians. Instead, they are the enemy who wished to oppress us, taking the place of the Dutch. Remember the tyranny of the Japanese occupation. Under the Japanese government, how hard our life was! Although they pretended to promote our independence, it was merely a trick to deceive and use the Indonesians. The Japanese had no actual intention of liberating Indonesia.

These kinds of comments simultaneously filled the front pages of various papers. In addition, news of the clashes between the Allied Forces and the Indonesians suddenly disappeared and exaggerated reports of small troubles between Indonesians and the Japanese began to appear. And, those essays or reports often included such strange opinions as "The Dutch government was much better than the Japanese government."

Although this was a brief statement inserted at the end of an elaborate discussion, it made me very fearful for the Indonesians, for I felt that this phrase was very dangerous to the future of Indonesian independence. It might have been true that in some aspects the suffering of Indonesians who were forced to share the hardships of the Japanese bitter efforts as they were losing the war, was greater than their suffering under the Dutch in peaceful times. We, ourselves, were falling in agony and death in the last part of the war. We therefore could not completely deny this statement. We Japanese, however, were afraid of the tense used in the statement. "The Dutch government was better than the Japanese government" might be switched from "was" of the past tense to "will be" of the future tense, if the stength of the Indonesians was consumed by useless conflicts with the Japanese. This could lead the Indonesians on a dangerous course. We felt that the clever strategy of NICA was behind such a charge.

As it turned out, in early November, the chief of NICA in Sumatra, Lt. Col. Knottenbelt, visited the Acehnese capital, Kota Raja, and interviewed several leaders of the Ulebalang class. Although the content of the conversation was unknown to us, we were very surprised by the sudden change of attitude of one of the Ulebalang. Coming out of the interview, he said, "The Dutch government was better than the Japanese government."

Such a statement was never anticipated from this person because he had been one of the most active cooperators with the Japanese ever since we landed. We admired the cleverness of Lt. Col. Knottenbelt, though the Ulebalang who made the comment was soon after killed by Acehnese youths.

In the Medan area, however, the Indonesian papers continued to focus crazily on the faults of the Japanese military government, never paying attention to the above-mentioned danger. We could not necessarily conclude that the newspapers were really affected by the Dutch, because newpapers tend to like something new and exciting. The papers may have jumped at a new idea scattered by some secret agents.

We thought at that time only of the strategy of NICA. However, there was another possible source, the strategy of the underground Communists, because the change occurred just when the youth party was reorganized as the Socialist Youth tionalists and Communists had cooperated in the independence movement since the colonial period. But their aims were different. As said in China, "*Dosho-Imu*" (different dreams in the same bed), the Communists dreamed of world communism as the final goal instead of the independence of a nation. Consequently they disliked the nationalistic independence dreamed of by the Japanese. They scattered stories containing false information -- that the Japanese were attacking Indonesians -- to incite the active Indonesian youths to murder Japanese. When the Japanese counterattacked, they publicized only the Japanese attack. Most Indonesians in Java thus began to think the Japanese were their enemy. This hostility toward the Japanese seemed to be spreading to Sumatra. The Communists and NICA also dreamed the same dream in different beds.

Anyway, the strange smoke of anti-Japanese sentiment was fanned out from an unknown fire and rapidly spread, cleverly hiding the poison gas of the pro-Dutch.

The situation for the Japanese worsened day by day. Pesindo placed their sentries in the Medan Telephone Station and communication in the Japanese language was often disturbed. Threatening letters were repeatedly delivered to our liaison office telling us, "We shall raid your liaison office at 9 o'clock this evening. If you resist, we shall kill you all."

In great fear our liaison office reinforced its defenses. An interpreter from our office disguised himself as an Indonesian and investigaged the atmosphere in the streets. He found only increasingly anti-Japanese voices. Our office was in constant fear of being raided. With an air of tragedy, we reinforced our defenses by charging the barbed-wire barricade with electricity and increasing the number of sentries. However, the power of less than a hundred people, including unarmed civilians, was never thought to be sufficient.

ANTI-JAPANESE VOICES

These days, I visited the house of the intelligence unit of the Fifth Corps almost every evening because I could not go out at night without risking my life because of the martial law imposed by Allied Forces, as well as the Indonesian hostility towards Japanese.

Their house was the third one from the corner of Serdang Street and was of European style with white mortar walls. It was surrounded by a low hedge and had an entrance and a small lawn on the right side. The door of the house and a terrace faced the right side garden. Inside the door was a big room with several sofas. This was the meeting room of the youths. When I came in, someone usually stood up to give me a welcoming seat.

Public opinion was immediately reflected in the attitudes of the young people in the intelligence unit. I found their feelings were moving parallel with the tone of the newspapers or the voices in the streets. The bad memories of the Japanese, which had been sleeping in the bottom of their hearts, now suddenly surfaced in their brains. One night when I joined their conversation, they began to focus on the faults of the Japanese one after another. Ismed opened the charges:

"The Japanese military police (MP) were very dangerous. An Indonesian I know was arrested by the MP on suspicion for something of which he was completely innocent. He was tortured by beating and kicking for more than half a day to get him to confess. When he was released after being proven innocent, he was almost half dead, and remained in bed for nearly a month afterwards."

Bob followed Ismed: "It is true. We Indonesians were always in mortal fear of being informed on to the MP. Once a person was accused on suspicion, he would be tortured until he said, 'I am sorry for that,' regardless of whether he did or didn't do it. He would be tortured to death if he did not say anything. Since the emissaries of the MP were uneducated, low-class Indonesian thugs, it was never known what they would tell the MP if a person were to irritate them. If an emissary of the MP stopped a person asking him to lend him his bicycle, he could not refuse. No-one could dare be bold enough to ask if the bicycle would be returned. When a maid at the MP station wanted to buy some vegetables at the market, no-one could dare ask her to pay."

I knew this to be true. When the MP appointed any of the Indonesians to be an emissary of the MP, the emissaries were hardly secretive and wielded outrageous power over those Indonesians who feared the MP. Spies of the Allied Forces, approaching the coast in submarines, were able to land secretly in Sumatra in rubber boats, because, in the last part of the war, there were many betrayals in response to the weakening of Japan. The Japanese MP desperately searched for these traitors, but, in the final analysis, their efforts were ineffective and served only to spread useless fear among the inhabitants. The flashing signals from the enemy submarines communicating with the spies on the land continued to blink in the darkness of the Malacca Straits as if they were ridiculing the Japanese MP.

As soon as Bob finished his talk, Nirwan leaned forward, full of resentment: "One evening, a drunken Japanese officer came to my house. He ate and drank, roaring, 'Bring water,' 'Give me tea,' etc. On seeing the figure of my sister in an inner room, he said, 'Hey, is that your sister? Lend her to me for a night.' I answered him angrily, losing all patience, 'If I visit your home in Japan and ask you to lend me your sister, would you be willing to lend me your sister?' I risked my life daring to respond in this way. The officer fortunately left blushing. The officer was better than some other Japanese drunkards. The Japanese drunkards were very difficult for us to host, since they carried long swords."

I had no reason at all to refute him. There were many Japanese who became like that when drunk, despite usually being gentle. How dreadful the Japanese common saying was, that praised the moral paralysis of drunkeness as leading to a joyful frankness! How dreadful it was for the inhabitants when the people who could become crazy at any time were carrying the swords of a supporting military power!

The usually soft-spoken Jusuf also edged himself into the conversation: 'The Japanese administrators were really funny. Really. They gave complimentary tickets to the movies only to the Eurasian girls of Dutch nationality if they were pretty. We Indonesians who were the best allies of the Japanese were not given even a single ticket. While the girls of the enemy nation were comfortably watching the movie in the reserved seats, we Indonesians could only get the low-class seats while still paying an awfully expensive price as a premium. For an especially good movie, we could not get even the low-class seats."

In China, an extraordinarily pretty woman is called "*Keisei* (castle decliner)," because throughout history, even powerful men often lost their castles by loving such beauties too much. It seems to be an inevitable part of human nature to be attracted by a pretty woman, in spite of oneself. Even I, myself, was somewhat ashamed to hear Jusuf's words, though I listened pretending to have no guilty conscience. Ismed once again criticized the Japanese:

> The Japanese were always proud of being Japanese and despised Indonesians generally as natives, lumping the educated and uneducated together. You were the only Japanese who associated sensitively with us, respecting us as equals. All of us here were educated in high schools or colleges. We do not believe that we are inferior to most Japanese, who despise us as natives. We believe that we are superior to the uneducated Japanese in both knowledge and culture. In the administration, they forced unreasonable policies upon us without first studying the customs and society of the inhabitants. If we criticized such an administration even a little, the military police would immediately label us as anti-Japanese. When we had some opinions, we could tell them only to you without fear. By oppressing the minds of the people in such a way, the administration could never be reasonable."

As Ismed claimed, the pride of the Japanese people rested on too hollow a base. We Japanese lacked too much in wisdom and generosity to govern other races. Pane, too, joined in the criticism: "The distribution of tobacco was also unfair. Good tobacco was never delivered to the natives. The rationed clothes were also largely usurped by the Japanese administrators to sell to the Chinese or to give to the Eurasian girls. It was unspeakably unfair."

The ten youths who were present competed with each other in blaming the Japanese in this way. Listening in complete silence, my head began to ache. There was no use denying anything, because all their claims were true. Before hearing the present claims, I already knew of such things.

Essentially, I do not think that the Japanese slogan of Asian Liberation was a lie. The reason why so many of us Japanese youths were ready to devote our lives to the war was because of our passion for the mission to liberate our Asian people. For many years we had been angry at the colonization of Asia by the Europeans. On the other hand, however, the prosperous bonanza of the British and Dutch colonial empires made us envious, and we could not completely deny our wish to take the same privileged place. Consequently, even among those of us who wished to be saviors, there were more than a few who did not respect the natives as humans, and despised them in the same way as the European conquerors.

In addition, the desperate efforts of the Japanese in the last moments before surrendering inflicted upon the native inhabitants unmeasurable torments, both physically and spiritually. We Japanese have done many of the things for which they are now blaming us. We must apologize to them with our heads deeply, deeply bowed. Even in the present anti-Japanese storm being carried out by the Indonesians, we are not qualified to blame them in return.

The youths who surrounded me with their accusations toward the Japanese were affected and excited by their own words, being borne along on a contagious stream of anti-Japanese sentiment together with the public. Their hearts were now filled with the bad memories of the Japanese and had no space to admit the good memories that they had appreciated during their pro-Japanese period. With no energy in reserve to try to refute them, I listened in silence, allowing them to speak without any reservation.

When they finally tired of their accusations, I opened my mouth for the first time and said to them quietly: "It is perfectly true that the Japanese have done those things. I, myself, have heard of those deplorable things. It is quite natural for you to bear grudges against the Japanese; your hearts are full of grudges. You have good reason."

They were, however, intelligent youths. Noticing my deep sadness, they came back to themselves with a start, answering:

> Oh no. Of course, we remember many favors we were given by the Japanese too. The Japanese gave us the courage to stand up and request equality with the Europeans by defeating the Dutch. All

Indonesians could become one nation for the first time during the Japanese administration. The Japanese trained us in the military and administrative affairs that prepared us for independence. We know that. But, we cannot help being angry, because the Japanese blame us Indonesians for being brutal, ignoring their own past misdeeds because we are persecuting the Japanese a little now. It is your turn now. Since you are the best friend of the Indonesians, please point out all the badness of the Indonesians without reservation. We are close friends. Let us listen now. Let us help each other by pointing out each other's faults.

Although they thus urged me to accuse the Indonesians in return, I was too tired. My heart was full of regrets for the faults of the Japanese occupation and I had no others. So I stood up saying, "I am sorry, but listening to you has exhausted me. I have no more energy left. Let me talk next time."

I was very tired, with an ache in the bottom of my heart. The young men simultaneously stood up and bowed, seeing me off.

The youths of the intelligence unit, who were always sympathetic toward me, initially said when our liaison office received a threatening letter, "Tell us when the robbers are attacking your liaison office. We will drive them away." When the situation got worse, however, they said: "In the current situation we are no longer able to protect your liaison office. If we dare try, we ourselves risk being labeled as traitors. If the Indonesians attack your office en masse, we will bring you alone to a safe place. Please trust us. We will make every effort to save your life."

I, however, refused their kind offer: "Thank you, but no. You do not have to save me. If all my comrades are being killed, I do not wish to be the only one saved. I am one of the Japanese. If you Indonesians really hate and want to kill the Japanese, I am ready without hesitation to be killed along with my comrades."

"Because you are such a person to say so, we are even more anxious to save you." Saying this, they respected me even more. My reason for saying what I did, however, was not mere gallantry. I knew that even if I were saved, I would not be secure in the midst of such an anti-Japanese storm.

THE JOINT DECREE

Under such circumstances, on December 5, the 26th British division commander in Bukit Tinggi, who was responsible for Sumatra, issued a curious Allied Forces-Japanese Joint Decree. It appeared in the newspapers as following: "The Japanese Army is responsible for the administration and social order of all Sumatra, except the Medan-Belawan area that is directly controlled by Allied Forces."

However, it was impossible for the Japanese to respond to such a decree. In the surrender agreement made in Rangoon immediately after the war's end, the Allied Forces ordered the Japanese forces to maintain social order in the occupied territories until the administration was returned to the Allied Forces. Here in Indonesia, however, the Indonesian people had proclaimed independence and established their own government organization. Since the surrendering Japanese forces had completely lost the respect of the inhabitants, they had no power to intervene in domestic administration, and no will to do so either. In addition, it was thought impossible for the Japanese to transfer administration to the Allied Forces if they were unable to leave the limited area of Medan-Belawan. The agreement had already become a dead letter, without any realistic means to fulfill it, at least in Indonesia.

Because the Indonesian government was fortunately following the same organization as the Japanese administration, the Japanese army had left some Japanese officials in nominal positions, such as provincial Residents, controllers, and others, while giving actual sovereignty to the Indonesian officials, pretending to rule indirectly through them. Therefore, no change in the actual behavior of the Japanese was possible despite the announcement of the decree. This fact was understood by the British who were always very pragmatic.

Unfortunately, however, the Indonesians did not take it that way. They were afraid that, if the Japanese were to follow the decree literally, the Japanese would be obliged to reestablish the military government, denying Indonesian independence and oppressing the Indonesians by military force. Although the Japanese had no desire to do so, the decree was unfortunately a joint statement co-signed by the 26th British-Indian Division commander and the 25th Japanese Army commander. As a result, the Indonesians took it as a declaration by the Japanese army of their intention to suppress the independence movement. The Indonesian newspapers explained the decree as follows:

> Following the order of the Allied Forces, the Japanese forces have finally decided to destroy Indonesian independence. The Japanese are no longer our friends. Instead, they are the cat's paw of the Allied Forces.

The eyes of the Indonesians watching the Japanese suddenly turned bloody. Although Indonesians had already been generally anti-Japanese, most of them had not gone beyond pointing out the faults of the Japanese occupation. But now, they began to call Japanese their enemy.

According to international law, it was actually impossible for the Allied Forces to order the Japanese to attack the Indonesians. An international treaty, agreed upon in The Hague immediately after World War I, prohibited the military use of the surrendering enemy. That is why, when our 4th Imperial Guard Infantry Regiment was ordered to advance to Aceh, the Allied Forces had to order only the restoration of social order and the return of weapons. They could not order an attack on the Acehnese. When I pointed out that the order to advance would actually mean an order to fight, the British withdrew the order. This was because the British were afraid of violating international law.

Because I had some knowledge of international law through reading an English text book at the liaison office, I believed that we Japanese could certainly avoid an attack on the Indonesian people that we did not want because of this international law. Beyond that, however, I was more afraid of the type of careless challenge to the Japanese by the Indonesians such as happened in Java. The Japanese would be obliged to respond, if the Indonesians attacked them first. Observing the response of the Indonesian people to the joint decree, I was deeply afraid of a challenge from the Indonesians.

In analyzing the situation, we began to realize the purpose of the decree that was announced, but that anticipated no action. We, the liaison officers, were deeply angry, assuming that this decree was made at the request of the Dutch. But we had no countermeasure. It was believed that the Dutch expected, first of all, that the foolish Japanese would suppress the Indonesian independence movement by following the decree literally.

Even if they did not fall into that trap, the Dutch expected that the Indonesians would be so irritated as to challenge the Japanese, and thus invite a counter-attack. When observed objectively, it was an admirably clever strategy.

We, however, could not remain spectators and simply admire such cleverness. Once an Indonesian-Japanese conflict resulted, it would be fatal to both sides. As the liaison officer managing Indonesian affairs, I stressed the meaningless of the joint decree to every Indonesian that I met, saying: "Despite the joint decree that was announced after the actual government was already in the hands of the Indonesians, we Japanese have no desire to intervene in the Indonesian administration. We Japanese have no intention of suppressing Indonesian independence."

The effect of such an effort, however, was quite limited because we, as the defeated enemy, were not permitted to use mass communications. If we were to make a public announcement, we would be accused of war crimes.

AN INTERVIEW WITH SIHITE

Soon after my arrival at my new post in the Medan liaison office, the power of the Fifth Corps reached its peak. Although we did not know how and by what means he could succeed, Sihite, the head of the Fifth Corps, was also appointed as chief of Pesindo. Sihite's power as commander of both Pesindo and Pasukan Kelima was literally like a rising sun, and he was reputed to be more powerful than either Governor Hasan or the TKR division commander, Col. Tahir. The youths of the intelligence unit of Pasukan Kelima were in extremely high spirits.

I thought that there was no person other than Sihite who could prevent a dreadful Indonesian-Japanese conflict. So I said to the youths of the intelligence unit: "I would like to meet your commander, Sihite, to find an effective way of preventing an unfortunate conflict between the Indonesians and Japanese. If Sihite is as respectable a man as you believe, he should understand my wish. Please contact him to set up an interview with me."

I was, however, told that getting in contact with Sihite was not easy because he was always moving around quickly and secretly. Losing my patience, I tried to threaten the youths and rejected their excuses. "Why does Sihite not want to meet me? A useless conflict with the Japanese would inflict serious damage on the Indonesian side also. I want to see him for the sake of Indonesians too. If Sihite does not really want to see me, we will be obliged to label Sihite as a tool of NICA, as is said in the rumors. Please tell Sihite this and bring me his answer."

Sihite was most afraid of such a label. Sihite, who despised the Japanese, was afraid of nothing else. Labeling him a tool of MCA could be fatal for him. Probably for that reason, Ismed of the intelligence unit finally brought me a message that Sihite was ready to meet me.

The security around him was extremely tight because he was afraid of attack from competing parties. Accompanied by two youths, I left the liaison office alone for the headquarters of the Fifth Corps. It was located on an avenue parallel to Lombok Avenue, two blocks east. When the inhabitants along the road saw an unarmed Japanese officer accompanied by the youths of Pasukan Kelima, they entered their houses hurriedly and watched me with pity through their doorways. We advanced along the quiet asphalt road, our shoes making a faint sound. When I turned the second corner, I found a crowd of Batak fighters on the avenue. On both sidewalks, the youths of suicide squads, some wearing the black shirts, stood in lines holding various weapons. We marched down the empty roadway in complete silence. Sihite was watching us from afar, standing in the center of the road, accompanied by several followers, large and small.

I approached the man who appeared to be Sihite and shook his hand. Following him, I passed through a hedged entrance and up the front steps. I took a chair and looked silently at Sihite across a big table in the center of a wide room. Sihite was a man of medium build and looked expressionless and strong-minded. He wore a military officer's green trousers, a black jacket, and a showy red-brown necktie. The room had no decoration and was furnished with another table with several chairs scattered randomly. The ceiling was dirty with cobwebs. I remembered a young Eurasian widow had lived in this house with her children before the war ended. Retaining no sign of its former occupant, the gloomy room was filled with a smell of cheap brandy. Broken bottles and glasses were in a corner. An old drunk sat on the seat next to mine, and poured unintelligible Batak words into my ear, together with the smell of brandy. Though it was very unpleasant, I calmed myself, thinking that I must control my temper to make the interview a success. Sihite's followers were watching my reaction from the other table. Each of them had a pistol at his waist. Ignoring the drunk by my side, I started to talk immediately, pulling my chair slightly forward towards Sihite.

In the poorly lit room, watching for a reaction in the depth of Sihite's eyes, I tried to persuade him in not very fluent Indonesian:

> I regret that our surrendering Japanese army cannot assist your independence movement because it is prohibited by the Allied Forces. We will, however, never attack the Indonesians. From the bottom of our hearts we sympathize with the Indonesians, because Indonesians and Japanese are related by blood. A strange rumor is being spread these days. If we brothers are deceived by it and struggle with each other, both Indonesians and Japanese will suffer serious misfortune. By all means we must prevent an unfortunate conflict between brother nations.

After explaining my basic position in this way, I emphasized the need for cooperation: "The danger of a struggle between brothers is already near. To prevent it, I need your cooperation, as the person who has the most influence among Indonesians at this time. In my present position as a defeated Japanese, I can only say that I ask you for the security of the Japanese. But, please understand, this is necessary also for independence."

Sihite, who had been listening in silence, finally answered: "I previously worked for the Japanese in the construction of air fields. Almost all the air fields in northern Sumatra were constructed by me as the contractor. There is no reason why I should be hostile toward the Japanese. I understand your meaning very well." Sihite's face was expressionless as he said this.

The drunk who was smelling of brandy by my side suddenly began crying, continuing to provoke me, while I kept calm showing neither fear nor anger. He bowed repeatedly to me, crying some unintelligible words and then he kissed my cheek, embracing me from the side. It was very unpleasant. A sticky kiss by a brandy-smelling old man can never be pleasant. I calmly stood up without even wiping the alcohol-smelling saliva from my cheek and walked down the front steps after shaking Sihite's hand. Sihite also came out to see me off.

The youths of the suicide attack squad, who were watching the result tensely from the sidewalk, simultaneously stood up and observed Sihite's and my face curiously. Both Sihite and myself were completely expressionless. I wished to smile a little to show my peacefulness, but the dried film of the brandied saliva from the old man seemed to be preventing the movement of my cheek muscles. I left the headquarters of the Fifth Corps with intentionally slow steps, looking back at the faces of the suicide attackers as they gripped spears, rifles, and other weapons.

When I turned a corner feeling many eyes on my back, I felt a line of chilly sweat streaming down my spinal column. By walking for a while, putting my strength into my abdomen and crying "I am not afraid" in my heart, I felt the sweat gradually become warmer. It was very unpleasant. I could not even swallow my own saliva because I felt as if the old man's saliva sticking to my cheek was penetrating into my mouth through the cheek muscle. Tightly closing my mouth, hurrying in my heart yet slow in my external actions, I came back to Lombok Avenue to the liaison office.

As soon as I arrived at the liaison office, I went directly to the *kamar mandi* (Indonesian-style bathroom) behind my room with my mouth tightly closed. Then I washed my cheek, spat out my saliva and gargled noisily with water. I was thus almost relieved and took a bath to remove the unpleasant memory.

However, I still could not confirm the true mind of Sihite. At least to me, it seemed impossible even for Sihite to take a pro-Japanese stance immediately. If he were to express a pro-Japanese attitude in the current atmosphere, he might possibly risk falling from power. Was Sihite a real freedom fighter or a secret tool of NICA? Was Sihite pro-Japanese or anti-Japanese? I failed to answer this question because I had been unable to see his mind through his clam-like eyes in this short interview. I thus remained suspicious of Sihite.

CHAPTER EIGHT
THE OUTBREAK OF THE TEBING INCIDENT

AN INCREASINGLY STRAINED SITUATION

The atmosphere became even more tense. Because seven Japanese managers disappeared on the Delitua Estate, all Japanese were ordered to retire from the estates around Medan. A group of 20 Japanese, including civilians who were retiring from the estates and sick soldiers, led by Major Takeuchi -- paymaster of the division headquarters -- left Medan for Malihat Estate in one car and two trucks. When they did not arrive in Malihat, our liaison office discovered that they had been captured by Pesindo in Sungai Rampah and were being held in prison. At the request of 2nd Lt. Honda, who used to be a trainer for the Indonesian volunteer army, TKR headquarters in Medan sent troops in, armed with machine guns, and rescued them.

That evening, a telegram from our divisional headquarters gave me the following order:

> The Imperial Guard Technical Regiment stationed in the Rambutan Estate discovered by secretly intercepting the Medan-Tebing Tinggi telephone cable that the Indonesians are planning an attack on the Japanese in Tebing Tinggi. Do your best to prevent this attack.

I immediately visited the Sumatran government to ask them to stop the attack. The government people tried every possible means to calm the youths but it had no power to control them. As a result, I looked for Sihite, who was now commanding the youth party in all of East Sumatra, to ask him to stop the attack. But I could not find out his whereabouts, because he kept his movements secret.

Telephone communication became impossible because the Indonesians had disconnected all the telephone cables between Japanese troops. On December 12, a wireless telegram from our division headquarters reported disturbing news. A train transporting Japanese civilians to the Dolok Sinumban Estate was being held in Tebing Tinggi Station and plundered by Indonesian youths. A lieutenant commanding the guard unit had been captured by the youths and his whereabouts were unknown.

Meanwhile, another serious telegram arrived from our division. Sixty soldiers headed by Capt. Iio, who were staying in Tebing Tinggi to purchase food and other supplies for the 5th Imperial Guard Infantry Regiment, had disappeared, with no news from them since last night. There were serious fears for their safety, but no details were known because telephone communication was blocked.

The Indonesian newspapers were still fervently anti-Japanese. Transportation between our liaison office and the Japanese troops outside Medan was completely blocked. Our liaison office with less than a hundred members was isolated in Medan where anti-Japanese propaganda was raging. Although the Allied Forces stayed close in the city, we could not expect their troops to be willing to help us at their own risk if we were attacked. A threatening atmosphere surrounded us. Charging the barbed wire barricades with electricity, we prepared for the worst.

THE INDONESIANS AND JAPANESE FINALLY CLASH

Because I was worried in particular about the situation in Tebing Tinggi, I asked the youths of the intelligence unit to investigate the situation there for me by telephone.

On the evening of December 13, his face dark with anxiety, Ismed of the intelligence unit came into my room in a flurry and cried in an astonished voice: "Good Heavens! I am so surprised. The telephone operator in Tebing was a Japanese soldier. The Japanese army has occupied the city of Tebing Tinggi! The Japanese and Indonesians are fighting each other in Tebing Tinggi."

I stood up, amazed. What I was most afraid of, had finally happened. At my wit's end, I could do nothing other than moan, clenching my fists, "Oh, my. Nothing helped. It finally happened."

Late into the night, a telegram was sent from division headquarters.

The massacred bodies of Captain Iio and other soldiers had been found in the city. The 5th Infantry Regiment had mobilized a battalion and was sweeping the rioters.

The commander of the 5th Infantry Regiment stationed in the Tebing Tinggi area was Maj. Gen. Shunpo Sawamura, who was promoted from colonel to major general at the end of the war. He had been venerated by the civil administrators of the military government as well as by the Japanese merchants, because he did not despise the civilians even though he was a professional military person. When I was an officer of the divisional communications troop, I was once invited by this regiment to teach them the construction of telephone lines. He always respectfully listened to me, though I was much younger and of much lower rank than he. He gave me the impression of being quite warm and sincere. When I visited him to ask for his support for my proposal to withdraw the disarmed Japanese from Aceh last month, he sincerely sympathized with my effort to prevent a bloody struggle between the Japanese and Acehnese, and generously assisted me. That this general had ordered an attack despite his pacifism indicated that there must have been no other option.

What I was most afraid of had finally happened. Even the British and Dutch forces did not order the Japanese to attack the Indonesians, though we suspected they wished to do so. The Indonesians themselves had invited the attack. The struggle between brothers, that I had prevented in Aceh in a desperate effort of cooperation with Governor Hasan, happened in East Sumatra Province, close to Medan. I was helplessly discouraged and confused.

It was reported that the battle was continuing in Tebing Tinggi. If this battle were to spread, what would happen? The unprotected Japanese soldiers, who had been disarmed by the Acehnese -- reputed to be even rougher than the Batak of East Sumatra Province -- would become hostages in a very dangerous situation. Noticing how powerless the effort of a small individual was in face of the larger stream of history, I completely lost the confidence that I had recently acquired.

SUMMONING MY COURAGE FOR THE WORST

The whole of Medan was thrown into great confusion the next day. The newspapers had blazing headlines such as "Japanese attack Indonesians.

The battle continues."

Seeing the roughly printed letters on the coarse paper manufactured for the first time by the Indonesians themselves using the paper-making machines brought by the Oji Paper-Manufacturing Company in Japan, I felt as if the newspaper reporters' anger spluttered through at me between the printed letters:

> In surrendering to the Allied Forces, the Japanese forces have become a tool of the Allies, and are trying to destroy the independent Indonesian Republic. The Japanese are our enemy. They are killing us.

The streets were full of such cries and the atmosphere was horrible. I was afraid our end was near. The situation was heading in the worst possible direction.

I spent one whole day in the depths of despair. On the morning of December 15, I went to the offices of the independent Sumatran government, summoning up my courage. Even under such circumstances, the Indonesian sentry did not bar my entry. Governor Hasan was away in Aceh, preparing for the peaceful withdrawal of the Japanese troops, in accordance with the agreement made with me. Maharaja Soankupon Siregar, the assistant governor, was sitting in the governor's chair. I approached this old friend of mine directly and proposed:

> What will happen if we cannot rationally solve this unfortunate conflict between the Indonesians and Japanese? We Japanese cannot allow Indonesians to kill us without doing anything. We cannot help defending ourselves if our lives are in danger. I cannot understand why Indonesians call the Japanese their enemy. Indonesians and Japanese have been brothers by blood for two thousand years. Who will be benefit if the brothers kill each other? There is not a moment to lose. Let us cooperate to stop the spread of this terrible situation.

Previously I had been especially close to Soankupon's family as if I were one of his relatives. Consequently, even in the middle of this anti-Japanese storm he warmly welcomed me and sincerely considered my proposal. He answered resolutely:

I agree with you completely. There is no reason why the Japanese and Indonesians must be enemies. However, the power of our government alone is not strong enough at the moment to solve this problem. It would be in vain if governmental officers were sent to pacify the situation. Let us do it this way. We shall hold a plenary meeting calling together representatives from all parties. After establishing a consensus that includes the opinions of the hot-blooded youths, we will find some way to solve the problem.

His analysis seemed excellent to me. There was not a moment to lose. I agreed immediately. Soankupon called to his secretary, "Call the Resident of Sumatra Timur!"

Tengku Hafas, the Resident of East Sumatra, came in hastily. A conclusion was reached between the two after a short discussion. Telephones rang simultaneously and messengers ran out in various directions to summon the party chiefs.

GALLANT PERSUASION

Very soon, the historical adventurers quickly arrived, one after another, and filled up a conference room in the upstairs of the Medan Higher Court. From the government, the acting governor, Soankupon, the East Sumatra Resident, Hafas, the provincial director of general affairs, and the chief of police, attended as the hosts. The acting TKR division commander, the police commander of TKR, a representative from Pesindo, the chief of the National Committee (KNI), the chief of the Nationalist party (PNI), a representative from the Communist party (PKI), the chief of the farmers' party, and others also took their seats. Total attendance numbered around forty. I sat in the next room listening to the conference through the glass windows.

Explaining the purpose of the conference, Soankupon, as chairman, expressed his opinion as follows:

Currently, the Japanese-Indonesian conflict is intensifying in many places. What kind of benefits are such conflicts giving to Indonesian independence? Until the war's end, the Japanese urged us to unite as one Indonesian nation and created various political and military organizations to prepare for our independence. Why must such Japanese be regarded with hostility now? What kind of benefits can we obtain by fighting with the Japanese? What will happen to our independence movement if we continue in this way?

Dear comrades. Why do you wish to intentionally fight the Japanese and regard them as the enemy? Why do you want to fight with them? The Japanese liaison officer, Capt. Fusayama, who deplores such a conflict between brothers, came to me to propose stopping the conflict. What do you think about it? Do you really want to make the Japanese our enemy?

Saying this he looked around the participants in a very determined manner. Soankupon's eyes were fiercely bright, though he was old. Soankupon, who used to be tottering with wrinkled eyelids, was now passionately watching the group, throwing his chest out and placing his fists firmly on the table.

Seeing this scene, I opened my eyes wide in surprise. How bold this pro-Japanese declaration was, in the midst of such a public anti-Japanese trend. It is easy for someone just a little clever to become a hero by standing at the forefront of the public grudge. But, an unusually resolute will is necessary to throw one's arms wide open against a raging public trend and cry, "Stop!" Deep respect and warm affection sprang into my heart. Tears almost fell from my eyes. Suppressed by the high spirit of Soankupon, none of the participants dared say, "I regard the Japanese as the enemy."

Soankupon pressed them further: "Well then. Let us save this very unfortunate situation as soon as possible through the cooperation of all parties and the government."

No-one dared oppose. But, the attitudes of the parties of varying positions and circumstances was as yet ambiguous. Agreement on a concrete plan was still difficult. The opinions of the party leaders, vacillating in line with the unstable tendencies of public feelings, repeatedly changed and reversed. The conference went on for four hours, without even stopping for lunch.

The final result of the conference seemed, however, to have been firmly established. Two days after Japan surrendered at the end of the war, Sukarno and Hatta proclaimed Indonesian independence with firm conviction; and the premise, "We must become independent and for that..," struck root in the hearts of a hundred million Indonesian people. In just the same way, the moment that Soankupon said, "the Japanese are no enemy" with firm conviction and no fear, the premise, "The conflict with the Japanese must be stopped," struck root in the heart of the participants. Although the details of the outcome could not be predicted, it had been fixed in principle. Because I was hungry and recalled a Japanese proverb, "If hungry, one cannot fight," I returned to our liaison office for lunch, fully trusting the leadership of Soankupon.

HESITATION BY THE INDONESIAN DELEGATES

When I was resting after lunch, the telephone rang and Soankupon told me, "We have decided that Resident Hafas and representatives of the principal parties will go to Tebing Tinggi for arbitration. They are meeting at Hafas' residence for their departure. I ask you to join the mission representing the Japanese."

I consented with great pleasure. When I was preparing for departure, the phone rang again and I was told, "We can arrange only one car due to the difficulty of getting tires. Can you please arrange two cars from the Japanese side?"

Sumatra was famous for producing crude rubber but had no refinery. Since the latter stages of the war when transportation from Japan was blockaded by the Allied Forces, the shortage of tires had become serious. After the war's end, tires were secretly imported but the black market price was tremendous. The finances of the independent government were too small, because of an inconsistent tax system, to buy new tires. Since I knew this well, I was obliged to agree. But arranging two cars was not easy, even for me.

If we were to go to Tebing in the middle of riots, the results would be uncertain. Only a few days previously, the three cars carrying the twenty Japanese under command of Major Takeuchi had disappeared on the way to Tebing Tinggi. The car-squad director was inclined to refuse unequivocally. After some negotiation I just managed to get his consent, but he canceled it soon after by telephone. Asking Major Imamura, the liaison office commander, to support me, I was able to borrow two cars after repeatedly going back and forth between the car-squad director and the liaison office commander. But there was only one soldier willing to risk his life and go with me as driver. Consequently, I asked the Indonesian government to arrange for an Indonesian driver for our other car.

Overcoming such difficulties, I barely arrived on time at the residence of Hafas. But only the provincial directors of general affairs and police affairs were waiting there and no delegates from the various parties had appeared. Because the TKR commander was ill, the chief staff officer, Lt. Colonel Sucipto was going in his place, but he telephoned to say that he could not come because he had to attend to a riot in Medan. No communication came from the other delegates. Resident Hafas seemed nervous and his face turned pale.

Without knowing why, I felt that the situation was uneasy. The missing party delegates seemed to indicate danger. The attitude of the delegates representing Pesindo and Pasukan Kelima, with the most sensitive information network, was a barometer of the degree of danger. Though I did not know what was happening in Medan or Tebing, the absence of the other delegates seemed to suggest trouble. Hafas looked at me nervously. "What shall we do?"

Because the martial law curfew time was approaching, I answered, "Well, no results can be expected if we go without them. Let's change the departure time to 8 o'clock tomorrow morning. Please call them to confirm for tomorrow." I then returned to the liaison office.

While I was eating my supper, some detailed information came from the division headquarters by wireless. In Tebing, the Japanese army was fighting the Indonesian youths from nearby villages in an attempt to take back Tebing City. As we had imagined at Hafas' residence, the situation in Tebing was still dangerous.

Just after 8 o'clock the next morning, I went to the residence of Hafas but found no-one but the pale Hafas. He said, "I don't know what is the matter. The delegates from the parties have not come this morning either. A few from the government came, but they left a moment ago."

It still seemed a bad sign. I also left, asking Hafas to telephone me if they showed up.

THE SECRET PRESENT

At almost 10 o'clock I received a cheerful phone call from Hafas. "They have come. Will you please come too?"

As I was leaving the liaison office, Nirwan, the head of the intelligence unit and Soankupon's second son, arrived flustered at my office and said: "Tuan. I heard you are going to Tebing Tinggi. Are you leaving now? Please be very careful. If you go, please take a pistol with you. I know you are walking around outside without a pistol for self-protection. But don't think you can calm Indonesian youths by mere talk. If you try to manage the unreasonable radicals by talk, you will only be killed. There will be no other way out than to shoot if you meet enraged rioters. I came here because I am afraid for you. Please be sure to take a pistol with you. I wanted to accompany you for protection, but my father would not permit me to do so."

Nirwan knew that I was walking around Medan with no pistol for protection because I had many close Indonesian friends and could speak the Indonesian language. I thought that even a shot could not save me in the worst of situations, but, gratefully accepting Nirwan's kind advice, I hid a pistol under the carpet of my car. My comrades at the liaison office also gave me much advice and words of caution. But my heart was full of confidence, though I did not know why. I, myself, was more anxious about the safety of Soankupon. So I led Nirwan into my room and secretly gave him a pistol saying: "I am more anxious for the safety of your father than for myself. Please protect him with this pistol so your important father is not assassinated by a radical. However, please be careful. If the fact that I gave you this pistol became known by the Dutch, I would immediately be accused of war crimes. Since we do not know who and where the spies of NICA are, you should not disclose this, even to your friends. Please be extremely careful."

Nirwan hid the pistol in his pocket after pressing it to his breast, and thanking me, saw me off in tears.

TEBING TINGGI

When I arrived at the residence of Hafas, already there were Hafas (Resident of East Sumatra Province), Damrah (director of general affairs), Mas Sidar (director of the Police Bureau), Sucipto (TKR chief staff officer), Burhan (representing Pesindo), Munar (representing the KNI -- the political committee), and a representative of PNI -- seven Indonesian delegates in total. Noticing that Sihite was missing, I telephoned to the headquarters of Pasukan Kelima and, finding Sihite, urged his participation: "We cannot be effective if you are not there. You must join us because you are influential in both Pesindo and Pasukan Kelima."

But Sihite stubbornly refused: "I cannot go because of another incident somewhere else. I think it is enough that Burhan represents our party."

Although Sihite now commanded both Pesindo and Pasukan Kelima in Medan, in the peripheral areas the two organizations still competed with each other. He, himself, must know that. Any representative from Pesindo other than Sihite could not be influential with Pasukan Kelima on the periphery. So I once again urged him to join us: "I have asked for a delegate also from Pasukan Kelima. If you yourself cannot come, please send your vice-commander, Nainggolan."

Sihite, annoyed, rejected me again: "Nainggolan is also busy. Since Pasukan Kelima is a section of Pesindo, one person representing Pesindo is sufficient."

I thought to myself, "This man is not sincere." He neither attended the conference yesterday nor came here today. I concluded that he was not willing to retrieve the peace between Indonesians and Japanese. I thought, "Okay, if he is not willing I will not push him to join against his will. I will do it myself." When I thought this way, an indomitable spirit arose in my heart crying, "No need for Sihite," despite the fact that until a moment ago I had thought that Sihite's participation was indispensable.

I stood up resolutely, put down the phone, and left Medan with the seven Indonesian delegates. The three cars driven by one Japanese and two Indonesian drivers threaded their way through the barricades of trees cut down on the road and headed for Tebing Tinggi. I silently thanked the Japanese soldier driving my car for his devotion in driving 80 kilometers along a road controlled by the rioters. The soldier himself, however, handled the car without any appearance of tension, watching the road ahead.

AN OMINOUS SILENCE ON THE TEBING ROAD

The road to Tebing Tinggi was literally under the silence of death. All the doors of roadside houses were closed. Not even a single cat could be seen on the road. The three cars ran in complete silence along the no-man's road. Only the sound of the tires could be heard on the asphalt pavement. Even the leaves of the palm trees along the road made no sound nor waved.

At the village of Sungai Rampah, we stopped our cars for a while to assess the situation. Some ten stores lined both sides of the road and some thirty or more houses formed a village. Several days ago in this village, twenty Japanese soldiers, including Maj. Takeuchi, passed by and were captured by Pesindo and thrown in prison. When we came there now, not a single inhabitant appeared on the road.

When we got out of the cars and entered the village, only the surprised eyes of the inhabitants were peering at us from behind their half-closed doors. The village headman, the policemen, and the Pesindo youths were now gone. We found the prison behind the village where the soldiers had been held, but it was now completely empty, with the doors of all the cells open. The khaki-colored military car of Major Takeuchi was found pushed into a roadside bush.

The frightened air of the inhabitants was extraordinary. I, who had expected to be surrounded by Indonesian youths pointing spears, returned to my car on the highway wondering what the reason was for such an unexpectedly silent atmosphere. When our car engines started, the windows of the roadside Chinese stores opened slightly and numerous frightened eyes could be seen peering out.

After passing the village of Sungai Rampah, no sign of human presence was seen, even in the houses. Was it the calm before a storm, or after a storm, I wondered. We passed through no-man's villages and no-man's rubber plantations, the only noise that of our engines. The roadside grasses were also motionless in the midday tropical sun. Even groups of monkeys usually visible playing in the rubber trees did not appear today. The green cross flag indicating the liaison office flew from the front of my car as we moved forward, followed by the other two cars. Before long, we saw the roofs of Tebing Tinggi ahead.

TERROR IN TEBING TINGGI

The hut on the roadside before the bridge across the Padang River, where the Indonesian sentries had surrounded me with spears two weeks ago, was empty today. The entrance to the bridge was closed by a barricade.

The other end of the bridge was blocked with sandbags, through which the tip of a Japanese machine gun ready to fire could be seen. Behind the sandbags a Japanese officer was watching us through his binoculars.

Stopping our cars at a distance, I walked alone toward the barricade and told of the purpose for our visit. The barricade was opened by the Japanese soldiers and our cars proceeded into the city. In the city, the two-story shop houses lined both sides of the road, their gray walls gravely supporting their sooty tiled roofs. All the doors were closed and the red and white independence flags, that used to hang everywhere, had completely disappeared. A few people could be observed but no-one wore the red and white independence badge. What a change it was! In Tebing Tinggi, no trace of the independence movement remained, and all the inhabitants were trembling with fear.

The first thing I did was bring our mission to the headquarters of the battalion occupying the city. The battalion commander was Maj. Seno, with whom I had been well acquainted. I explained the situation to the commander and his staff.

While I was talking, I saw through a glass door a few dozen Indonesian youths sitting in the next room with their hands tied behind them. When I opened the door to observe them, their terrified eyes looked at me and a stir went around the room. I staggered back and closed the door, shocked by what I'd seen.

CHAPTER NINE
THE STORY BEHIND THE TEBING INCIDENT

A FRENZY OF ANTI-JAPANESE AGITATION

I came to understand the events behind the current situation in Tebing from listening to the reports told to me by various people there. Let me explain the story from the beginning.

About two weeks ago, in late November, public feeling in Medan toward the Japanese suddenly turned from sympathy to hostility. Reflecting this change, the attitude of the youth in Tebing became arrogant, and Pesindo proposed the following to the Japanese army who had thus far been guarding the Tebing area:

> Since Indonesia has become independent, we would like to guard our city ourselves. It is unreasonable that the entrances to the city be guarded by Japanese sentries. Please withdraw these sentries and leave the guard duty to the Indonesians.

The Japanese army, who believed the Indonesians to be their friends and were more concerned with farming for their self-sufficiency, had no strong desire to continue directly controlling local security and so immediately welcomed the request and withdrew their sentries. Indonesian sentries began to guard all parts of the city, which actually meant that the city was under the control of Pesindo. This was the start of the Tebing Tinggi incident.

It was on December 1 that I had happened to pass through a corner of Tebing Tinggi, crossing the Padang Bridge on my way to Medan to take up my position as liaison officer. If I had fallen into the hands of Pesindo when stopped by the spears of the Indonesian sentries, I would have probably been killed like other Japanese.

It was around this time that a few strangers came to Tebing from an unknown place and began some anti-Japanese agitation, informing the residents of the British-Japanese Joint Decree, which most of them had not known about. The strangers had argued: "The Joint Decree is clear proof that the Japanese army has become a tool of the Allied Forces and is planning to attack Indonesians and destroy the independence movement. The Japanese are no friend of the Indonesians. They are our enemy."

The people in Tebing, who had thus far believed that the Japanese were their friends, were surprised by this and began to become hostile toward the Japanese. In addition, a strange *sate* (barbecued skewered meat) dealer came to Tebing and stressed to all the customers buying his *sate*: "The Japanese army is preparing to attack Indonesian independence powers. This is confidential news from Medan. We should attack first and kill them before they attack us."

After agitating for a while in this way, the stranger disappeared. The youth of Pesindo, who were hot-blooded and passionate about independence, were easily deceived by this deliberate agitation strategy and became very upset.

From where, and by whom, these agitators were sent is not known. The Indonesian delegates who came with me from Medan believed at this time that they were spies sent by NICA. On the other hand, the 16th Japanese Army headquarters in Java had repeatedly sent reports warning that the radical Communists who were causing the Indonesian-Japanese conflicts in many places in central Java by spreading anti-Japanese propaganda, were secretly penetrating Sumatra.

The city of Tebing Tinggi became full of anti-Japanese sentiments. The Javanese girls who used to be the service girls for Japanese soldiers during the war were captured by Pesindo youths. Their clothes were torn off and they were dragged around the streets exposed and crying.

In such an atmosphere, no other party could continue with a stance of moderation. No room for choosing one's behavior existed, because "anti-Japanese" was defined as "patriotic" and "pro-Japanese" as "betrayal." With Pesindo running wildly in the lead, all the other parties could not help but follow. All Indonesians in the city floated on a gigantic wave of anti-Japanese sentiment.

ATTACKS ON JAPANESE TROOPS

The main forces of the 5th Imperial Guard Regiment who were responsible for the Tebing area, were farming on the Bahilang Estate, 5 kilometers southeast of the city. The exit from the estate to the main road was closed by Indonesian sentries and barricaded. On December 8, Pesindo declared an economic blockade against the Japanese and prohibited all merchants in the city from selling anything to them.

Pesindo cut all telephone cables to the Japanese troops at the telephone exchange station and planned to attack small groups of troops one by one after isolating them from each other. At the Matapao Estate, southwest of Tebing, three Japanese managers, who had absolute confidence in the loyalty of their farm workers, stayed on to cooperate with a group of twelve Japanese soldiers headed by Lt. Isoda. At the instigation of Pesindo, however, the workers underwent an abrupt change of heart. They killed all the Japanese in a sudden attack. This incident was, however, completely unknown to the other Japanese because all communications had been cut.

The next day, a troop of twenty soldiers from the Japanese air force staying at Bedagai, halfway along the road to Medan, was besieged by several hundred Indonesian youths armed with spears and mountain knives. An Indonesian policeman informed the Japanese controller in Tebing of this, but it was impossible for him to do anything because he was in bed suffering from asthma.

During the night, the Imperial Guard Engineering Regiment staying at the Rambutan Estate intercepted Indonesian communications between Medan and Tebing by putting a wire on the telephone cable running along the railroad behind the barracks. On the telephone, Pesindo in Tebing was asking for reinforcements from Pesindo in Medan for an attack on the Japanese, planned for the following night. The regiment immediately reported this by wireless to the divisional headquarters in the Malihat Estate, but there was no way to inform the neighboring Japanese troops because the telephone cables had been disconnected.

Tebing Tinggi: Central Square

The Barracks of Capt. Iio's Troops near the Railway Station

Tebing Tinggi Railway Station

In Tebing, meanwhile, a small group of Japanese troops led by Capt. Iio remained, not knowing about such a plan. It was a mixed group of sixty soldiers who had been sent from various units to buy food and other supplies. They lived in three houses between the railroad and the main road to Tanjung Balai, just north of the Tebing Tinggi station. All the members had been in close contact with the locals because of their trade and Capt. Iio, a mild person with many close friends among the local residents, was quite optimistic, even under such circumstances, and stayed on without thinking of withdrawing to join the main forces. They could never have anticipated the possibility of being attacked by the Indonesians who had been so friendly to them.

Regardless of his wishful thinking, the situation steadily deteriorated. The troops were no longer able to fulfill their function due to the economic blockade. No communication with the other Japanese troops was possible because the telephone cables had been cut. Indonesian sentries prevented them from moving anywhere in the city. They could not know the details of the changing situation because no salesmen visited them. The houses that could be seen from the square in front of the railway station had all closed their doors. The scared occupants occasionally came out to look in the direction of the Japanese troops but soon none of them appeared beyond the door. A ghostly atmosphere began to surround the troops.

BETRAYAL OF GOOD WILL

The day of December 10 had a horrible ending. Summing up the information from surivivors and others involved, the following seems to be the most likely course of events:

The big tropical sun sank calmly over the quiet roofs of the houses in Tebing, and over the papaya trees behind the houses on the west side of the road, staining the trailing clouds reddish yellow. Meanwhile, the almost full moon began to rise over the coconut trees spreading to the east beyond the railroad.

Shortly thereafter, the horrid sound of *tonton*, made by hitting a huge wooden trunk hung in a small hut, signaled that something was happening in the direction of the central square. The sound passed over the red-brick roofs and vibrated through the windless evening sky, spreading to the edge of town. Sounds in response also began to be heard from the suburbs.

The city, which had been silent in the darkening night, became enveloped in a grisly tension. Young men holding spears and rifles began to proceed to the central square, hurrying in twos and threes under the faint light of street lamps. Whatever was going to happen? The sixty soldiers were now completely alone in a city ruled by the Indonesian youths. If something was going to happen in this city hostile to Japanese, the target could not be other than the troop of sixty soldiers.

It was almost 8 o'clock. A group of Indonesian youths suddenly headed down the dark road towards the troops' barracks. A variety of weapons were reflected in the faint street light. The sentries in the barracks strengthened their defense of the front entrance, attaching bayonets to their rifles. The barracks were three modified private houses, defended with barbed wire stretched on wooden posts hammered into a low hedge surrounding the barracks. The crowd on the road grew bigger by the moment.

Meanwhile, a tall man who seemed to be the leader stood in front of the entrance barricade and shouted, "We are here to take your arms. Let me see your commander."

Capt. Iio came out to talk with the leader. The other youths, impatient with the talk, tried to go in by pushing aside the bayonets of Japanese sentries because they knew that the Japanese soldiers had no desire to kill Indonesians. The sentries resisting the invaders anxiously waited for their commander's decision, holding their unfired rifles with their teeth set.

Capt. Iio, an elderly, mild-hearted officer, was, however, still thinking of peace. Firing on Indonesians was prohibited by the regiment commander. On the other hand, handing arms over to the Indonesians was strictly prohibited by the Allied Forces. He probably thought to himself, as the Japanese troop commanders in Aceh did in a similar situation: "If we fight, no small number of people will be injured or killed on both sides. The regiment commander prohibits the killing of Indonesians. We must avoid with all our efforts the mutual killing of those believed to be our brothers. It is quite understandable that they need weapons for the independence war. They will calm down if our weapons are handed over. If we give them weapons we cannot avoid severe punishment by the Allied Forces, but I will take the responsibility. The trouble will be over if I sacrifice myself in this way."

He ordered his soldiers to surrender their weapons which amounted to only six rifles for this non-fighting unit. He then shouted to the crowd of youths, "All the weapons will be given to you. Be quiet! Calm down!"

Barely suppressing their indignation over being robbed of their weapons, the soldiers handed them over. Capt. Iio expected a grateful handshake from the Indonesians.

Unfortunately, however, the results betrayed his expectations. The youths rushed on into the camp searching for more weapons. Six rifles were a small number for the crowd and so the youths extended their demands to watches and other private possessions, and squabbles ensued. At this moment a gun was suddenly fired from behind the crowd. It was not known who fired but the sound immediately drove the crowd into chaos. Becoming irate, the Indonesian youths attacked the Japanese soldiers with the arms they had just given them.

Recognizing the danger, Capt. Iio ran to the back gate of the barracks crying "Run out the back way!"

The soldiers inside and outside the houses followed him and rushed to the railway behind the barracks. There was no time to check the fate of the soldiers embroiled with the invaders. Some thirty soldiers followed him, stealing south along the railway. The youths did not follow them, probably because they were busy seizing various goods in the barracks.

A MASSACRE IN THE DARK

The railway divided into several lines toward the station. To join the main regiment force in Bahilang Estate, the soldiers had to pass through the station yard to the south and cross the river surrounding the east and west sides of the town by a 30-meter long iron railway bridge. They knew that they would reach the road to Bahilang Estate by following the railroad for one more kilometer.

Fortunately for them, a cloud that had just appeared in the sky covered the moon and made it dark. In order to hide themselves from a light in the station house, the escaping group walked on the east side of an open freight cargo train with bated breath, nervous of the sound of their feet on the railroad gravel. Silently, the group directed by Capt. Iio advanced south, following the faintly shining lines of the railway.

The Tebing Tinggi Station

To the southeast of the station yard was the village of Kampong Pisang, surrounded by many banana trees. At the edge of the station yard, close to the faint window lights of the village, they found a locomotive shelter. Just as they were approaching the shelter an Indonesian sentry appeared by the side of the railway and challenged them with a rifle at the ready, "*Siapa itu* [Who is that]?"

The group simultaneously lay down on the railway lines. A Japanese soldier immediately crept forward like a leopard, embraced the sentry from behind, and took the rifle while silently holding the sentry down. The sentry was so shocked he lost his voice. They began to walk forward holding the sentry as a prisoner. When they had advanced about 30 meters, another sentry challenged them from the darkness in front of the shelter, "Siapa itu?"

His figure was invisible. They again rapidly lay down. The challenging voice called out for a second and third time into the darkness. They could not answer, of course. The sentry fired his rifle in a series of three shots breaking the silence. It was the emergency signal. When three challenges went unanswered it was the rule for sentries to signal an emergency by quick shooting. The sentry acted just as he had been taught by the Japanese army. At this moment, the captured sentry ran off screaming. Many dark figures ran out of the locomotive shelter and some of them fired in the direction of the soldiers.

Capt. Iio cried, "Run to the left!" He ran to the east across the railroad and passed through the banana and then coconut trees. The group followed behind him. Shortly after, they ran into a ditch-like marsh. The marsh was so deep with a very soft muddy floor that they sank waist-deep. Many youths shouting in Indonesian rushed out from the station house to the marsh. Surrounding the place, they then fired their rifles at random into the marsh. Since the Japanese soldiers were unarmed, they could do nothing except lie close to the edge of the marsh. Tragic moans began one after another. The young men from the central square also came rushing down. The area around the marsh was filled with madly excited Pesindo youths holding numerous spears and rifles. The merciless massacre known as the Tebing Tinggi incident was thus underway.

The Indonesians dragged the Japanese soldiers out of the marsh, peeled off their clothes, and tied them up naked. The soldiers who tried to run towards the coconut trees were killed by the spears of the surrounding Indonesians. A soldier who could barely run was shot by the rifle of a youth following him across a bridge. His body was kicked into the stream. The captured soldiers were brought into the town and shot the next morning in front of the public. Their bodies were cut into pieces and buried. The body of Capt. Iio was dragged about on the street by a rope to show to the Tebing residents.

When they heard of this incident, Japanese in the liaison office in Medan, who were surprised by the cruelty, said that such cruelty was possible because the youths were Bataks who used to be cannibals until early in this century. But I do not think so because I have studied the folklore of the Batak race. Batak cannibalism was a punishment inflicted on a felon and was precisely regulated by *adat* (customary law). They never massacred many people at once.

Throughout the world, in reality, massacres have occurred not only in Indonesia, but in many other places too. When we fought in China, Japanese soldiers under siege were often killed and cut into pieces by the Chinese due to some religious belief. Even Europe is no exception. In various religious wars and riots, Europeans and pagans from the Near East were also massacred. Russians, too, are reported to have massacred 500 Koreans by throwing them through holes in the ice of the frozen Amur River early this century. Any race of people can become crazy murderers when blinded by religion or ideology.

THE PILLAGE AND MASSACRES CONTINUE

Because of the complete shutdown of communication, Japanese in other places were not aware of this tragedy. The next day, December 11, another group of ignorant victims came to Tebing. About 300 Japanese civilians, administrators, and merchants were being transported by a specially arranged train from Medan to the Dolok Sinumban Estate, escorted by some twenty soldiers. When the train passed through Sungai Rampah, Tebing was informed. When the train arrived, it was surrounded and the escort unit was requested to surrender all their weapons.

The escort commander initially rejected this request and several hours passed by. However, since the driver of the train left after being threatened by the youths, the escort finally gave up and handed over their weapons. The youths then robbed the train as well. The unit was permitted to leave in the evening, but the lieutenant commanding the escort was taken away by the youths. (Local inhabitants later reported that he was shot in prison.) This incident was reported by telephone to the divisional headquarters in Malihat when the group arrived in Dolok Sinumban, and the headquarters immediately telegraphed our liaison office in Medan.

Later that evening, the Indonesians attacked more Japanese troops on the Gunung Pamera Estate, located halfway to Pematang Siantar. Because the 5th Infantry Regiment's food storehouse was located there, a group of nineteen soldiers, headed by 2nd Lt. Inoue, stayed there to guard the storehouse along with two Japanese managers. The workers on the estate were quite friendly to the Japanese. The policeman was also very close to them, often visiting the office to talk and laugh.

The peaceful atmosphere was suddenly broken that evening. The workers, who often used to visit, did not come. Many Indonesians gathered instead in the center of the estate, burning bonfires. The policeman, who used to be so friendly, assumed a completely different attitude and demanded: "We need weapons for independence. Surrender your weapons to us."

Lt. Inoue asked, "Whose order is this?"

The policeman answered, "Pesindo's."

Handing over weapons was, of course, strictly prohibited by the Allied

Force.

The soldiers, therefore, picked up their arms and took defensive positions. The crowd was growing. Indonesians surrounded the Japanese barracks holding bamboo spears and mountain knives. They began to throw stones and slowly crept closer to the barracks. The situation was becoming very serious.

Lt. Inoue telephoned the regiment's headquarters to ask for permission to shoot: "Numerous Indonesians are approaching and surrounding our barracks. Please permit us to shoot. Otherwise we cannot defend ourselves."

The regiment commander, Maj. Gen. Sawamura, however, did not grant permission. Instead he ordered Lt. Inoue to solve the dispute by negotiation. Meanwhile, the Indonesians cut the telephone cable. Inoue's platoon was completely isolated, unable to communicate with other Japanese.

It was impossible for the small number of Japanese soldiers to defend themselves against the overwhelming number of Indonesians without shooting. In addition, they no longer had the means to ask for help or consult with superiors. Having no other option, Lt. Inoue finally decided to surrender their arms to the Indonesians and ordered his soldiers to stack their weapons in front of the barracks.

The Indonesians watched them for a moment, not understanding at first what they were doing, but soon they approached. Just at this moment suddenly the sound of gunfire was heard behind the crowd, and someone shouted out. The shout appeared to be made by some secret agitator. In response, the Indonesians simultaneously rushed upon the Japanese soldiers, holding their native weapons high. Inoue cried, "Run away," and tried to escape with his soldiers, but nine of them were killed immediately.

Lt. Inoue ran out with several soldiers but they were soon caught by their pursuers. Inoue stopped suddenly and stood opening his arms wide to prevent the Indonesians from reaching his fleeing soldiers. An Indonesian youth attacked him frontally with a spear. Inoue grasped the spear as he dodged aside but cut his fingers. Another youth approaching from behind gave him a heavy blow on his head with a mountain knife. He fell, unconscious, with his head stained with blood.

The fire of his life was, however, not extinguished. After several hours, he regained consciousness after being washed by the cool night dew and found himself lying on the ground in only a loin cloth. The Indonesians had taken off all his other clothes. They left his body there, probably believing that he was dead. He then crept through the jungle and was fortunately rescued by an Indonesian farmer. He stayed at the farmer's house for several days until the Japanese army found him after the incident was over.

The regiment headquarters were unaware that such merciless events were happening in Gunung Pamera.

DEMANDING THE 5TH REGIMENT SURRENDER THEIR ARMS

On the morning of December 12, after such a wild night, a mission of several youths representing Pesindo visited the Bahilang Estate to see the regiment commander, pretending to be ignorant of the massacre. The young delegates spoke one after another:

> We have cooperated with the Japanese army, trusting your promise to support our independence. Japan lost the war. We started the independence war ourselves. You are, therefore, required to give us your arms since they are no longer necessary for you as the defeated party. We request you to hand over to us all the arms of the regiment. This Bahilang Estate is now surrounded by 3,000 of us. If you resist, we are ready to take them by force, killing all of you. Obey and surrender your arms before we attack you.

At that time, only 400 soldiers were there including the regiment headquarters, the communications company, and other directly controlled units. The majority of the regiment's forces were scattered in various other estates. The senior adjutant, Capt. Nakamura, who interviewed the Pesindo delegates for Maj. Gen. Sawamura answered resolutely:

> Our arms are our spirits of Samurai received from our Emperor. They cannot be handed over without orders from our superiors. The Japanese army promised in the surrender agreement to keep all arms until they are handed over to the Allied Forces. We cannot break that promise. If you were to attack, we will have no choice other than to

defend our lives.

He then protested the pillage of Japanese civilians that had occurred the day before at Tebing Station, and questioned the youths about the safety of the troops who had been reported missing in various places, particularly the troops commanded by Capt. Iio. The youths claimed they knew nothing about that, looking at each other. When they were about to leave after reaching no agreement, Adjutant Nakamura called them back and tried another proposal, "Bring the Japanese soldiers who remain in the city here to safety, and we will be ready to give you some arms secretly as a reward."

This was actually possible because the regiment had some unassigned arms for emergency use. The youths, however, left without responding to the proposition to trade, despite keenly wanting the arms.

The regiment reinforced their defenses by digging trenches around the estate, stretching wires charged with electricity, and cutting down rubber trees to open up the field of fire. A few of the Javanese workers on the estate were sent into the city to investigate the situation. They brought back the information that four Japanese officers who were traveling through Tebing had been captured and publicly executed. An Indonesian farmer living on the east side of the river informed them that he saw Indonesian youths across the river burying the bodies of three Japanese soldiers. Nothing, however, was known about the troops living close to Tebing Station. The evening of December 12 grew dark.

REPORT OF AN ESCAPE

In the dawn of December 13, an unbelievably peaceful morning was beginning to break, with the sunlight falling through the green leaves of the rubber trees over the guard house at the camp entrance of the 5th Infantry Regiment.

At that time, a blood-stained sergeant appeared like a ghost in the morning mist. He fell down after staggering into the guard house. He was raised up by the arms of the surprised soldier on guard. How tragic he looked. The tip of a native spear that had been stabbed through his back was exposed in his chest.

The regiment headquarters immediately fell into extreme chaos. The sergeant's pulse was taken by an army surgeon, and the wounded soldier desperately tried to move his jaw to tell of the tragedy that had befallen the Tebing troops. He was a member of Capt. Iio's troops, and reported the story of his escape as follows.

On the evening of December 10, when the incident started, the soldiers being attacked by the Indonesians ran out of the camp to the east. He ran at the tail of the group. When the group was found by the Indonesians in front of the locomotive shelter and Capt. Iio cried, "Run to the left," he ran to the east following his comrades. But they had run into a marsh covered by water grasses. In that instant he sank in the water up to his neck. He floundered about but could not pull his boots out of the mud. Because the Indonesians had come close, he hurriedly hid himself, covering his head with grass and holding his breath. The Indonesians began to snipe with their rifles at those who were trying to creep out of the marsh. He heard the screams of his comrades, as if it were a nightmare.

Meanwhile, the Indonesians dragged the survivors out of the marsh and took them toward the station house. They then returned to the marsh and walked around the edge, piercing all the grassy surface with spears to search for anyone remaining. Fortunately, however, the spears failed to catch him.

When the place was completely quiet, he drew his legs out of his boots that were still tightly stuck in the muddy floor and crossed the marsh in his bare feet. When he reached a comparatively high and dry place, after wandering endlessly through the dark coconut woods, he fell down, exhausted, and slept deeply.

When he woke in the morning sunshine, he found himself lying in a line of huge jars in a Chinese cemetery. It was the custom of immigrants from South China to leave a dead body in an open jar placed in the field and bury the bones in the earth when all the flesh had decomposed. When he woke up, his completely wet body was chilled, there was a pain in his abdomen, and he began to suffer from diarrhoea. But he could not move from there for a whole day because Indonesian youths with rifles or spears were coming and going on a path a short distance away.

When the sun was about to set, he staggered almost unconscious toward the village, because he could no longer stand the serious hunger, cold, and diarrhoea. An Indonesian child playing nearby noticed him and approached smiling. The child invited him to its house: "Sir. Japanese soldier. Come to my house."

He hesitated, not knowing what to believe. But an Indonesian woman, who seemed to be the child's mother, came out of the house and said gently, "It is dangerous for you to be out here. Come into my house quickly."

Although he could not understand the reason for her kindness, he entered the house because nothing else seemed possible. An old woman, probably the grandmother, was inside. The two ladies kindly took off his wet clothes, dressed him in a sarong and burnt some wood to warm him as he was shivering. After he greedily ate the warm, rice soup that was offered, he began to feel better.

According to the old woman, the father of the child was a policeman. Until the war's end, he was a Heiho working in the 5th Infantry Regiment. Because of his excellent record he was promoted to the position of squad leader. The grandmother said repeatedly: "My son was educated by the Japanese army as a Heiho and became a very reliable man. He was always thankful and respectful toward the Japanese. Please hide yourself until the danger is over."

The women washed and dried his soiled wet clothes and treated him warmly, occasionally telling him news from outside. Trusting their kindness, he stayed there for one whole day until the following evening. Indonesian youths, however, were searching for any remaining Japanese with increasing intensity. Japanese soldiers were being found one after another, and either captured or killed.

A SPEAR PIERCES HIS CHEST

The sergeant began to feel that even this house could not be safe for long. He also began to feel it his duty to inform his regiment headquarters of the tragedy. Late on the night of December 12, he left the house quietly and began to pass through the coconut woods towards Bahilang Estate. He reached the railway bridge over the river but it was guarded by an Indonesian sentry. He turned west through a plowed field and came to the southern end of Tebing City.

There was a road that he often took to go the regiment headquarters. At the place where the road left town, crossing the river, there was an arched stone bridge that was rare in Sumatra (this bridge was later rebuilt with iron). It was a Chinese-style bridge, made by the local Chinese merchants. He would have to cross this bridge to get out of town. The moon was just coming out from behind a cloud and its light shone through the coconut trees onto the bridge. It was dangerous, but the shade by contrast was fortunately very dark. When he began to steal over the bridge, however, one of the Indonesian sentries watching the road to Bahilang Estate on the other side of the bridge, detected him and shouted, "Siapa? Siapa itu [Who's that]?"

It was all over for him. The road to Bahilang was closed by a barricade. Giving up the idea of going directly to Bahilang, he passed in front of the guard hut like a rabbit and ran desperately to the south on the road that led toward the town of Pematang Siantar.

On the moonlit road, there were neither houses nor trees to provide cover. He kept running down the straight road. His pursuers got closer every moment. The sound of feet and cries were behind him. He ran, his throat dry, concentrating all his energy. He knew there was a path off this road to Bahilang a short distance ahead. He could reach the road to Bahilang after passing through a rubber forest and crossing a small stream. Two kilometers from there would be the regiment. He ran desperately, his teeth set. The Indonesians, however, could still be heard pursuing him.

Just at that moment, another group of youths holding spears appeared in the moonlight ahead. The situation was desperate. The soldier dashed himself against a youth at one end and tried to escape like a cornered mouse. Unfortunately, as he tripped on the grass at the side of the road, a spear pierced him from behind. "Wah....!"

As he grabbed at it, the spear broke at the handle. With the tip piercing his chest, he fell into the roadside ditch. In contrast to the bright highway surface, the shaded drain was very dark. He lost consciousness. He was only 26 years old. He was now dying there, unbeknownst to any Japanese. His pursuers looked down at him for a while in the dark ditch and then left, believing him dead.

Miraculously, however, he was still alive. When he regained consciousness, it was already close to dawn and he found himself lying at the edge of some rubber trees beyond the coconut forest. How he got there he could not remember. The regiment headquarters must be nearby. With all his strength he struggled to walk and finally arrived at the guard house.

DECIDING TO RETALIATE

After hearing his report, regiment headquarters became aware of the tragedy that had befallen the soldier's unit. The information that the engineering regiment in Rambutan Estate had obtained by intercepting the telephone cable and had reported to the divisional headquarters was now confirmed. The Japanese who had been reported missing in various places had probably met with the same fate. Maj. Gen. Sawamura, the regiment commander, who had been so patient thus far, had at last run out of patience. The compassion and compunction he felt for his soldiers, who had been cruelly killed while restraining their fire in accordance with his orders, rested heavily on his heart. He reported the situation and his resolution to the divisional headquarters by wireless and asked the divisional commander for permission to attack the Indonesians. The surprised divisional commander sent a telegram to warn against such a rash act and sent his senior staff officer, Lt. Col. Muromoto, to Tebing in a hurry.

The Communist party in North Sumatra had not joined in the attack on the Japanese. Instead, it maintained connections with the divisional headquarters, expressing its willingness to cooperate. Since the road to Tebing under the control of the Indonesian youths seemed to be too dangerous for a Japanese car, Lt. Col. Muromoto used a Communist party jeep, for the journey.

In general, the behavior of the Indonesian Communist party in Sumatra toward the Japanese was completely different from that of the party in Java. The Communists generally did not like the fact that Indonesian independence was supported by the Asian nationalism of the Japanese, and in Java they sought to cause hatred and trouble between the Japanese and the local people. The Communist party in East Sumatra, however, had never caused any trouble for the Japanese. Instead, it had been cooperative. The head of the party was Abdul Xarim, a famous independence leader who had often been imprisoned by the Dutch. He was released by the Japanese army and became an active cooperator as the head of the Fatherland Defense Association to inspire Indonesians in Sumatra to patriotism and Asian nationalism, mobilizing young people for the defense services. When he became head of the Communist party after the war's end, all the Japanese were very surprised. But his party did not cause any trouble, unlike the Communists in Java. He was in reality a nationalist, and resisted Dutch colonialism as well as the control of the international Communists. He was, therefore, expelled by Communist headquarters in Java some years later.

Staff Officer Muromoto, arriving in Tebing, found the situation was much more serious than his division headquarters had guessed. It seemed difficult to sway the resolve of Maj. Gen. Sawamura, whose many beloved subordinates had been killed. In addition, it was believed that the Japanese would continue to be killed if no response was made to the massacres. Consequently, Lt. Col. Muromoto finally agreed that Tebing should be attacked. He reported his opinion to the division commander who responded by granting his permission. Maj. Gen. Sawamura immediately announced the order to attack. The soldiers of the 5th Regiment, who were watching this process with bated breath, simultaneously stood up in high spirits.

> His Excellency Sawamura has ordered an attack. The regiment commander, who thus far prohibited any attack, has finally given his permission. Comrades, be pleased. We will retaliate for you. His Excellency Sawamura has ordered retaliation at last.

At 3 o'clock on December 13, a battalion commanded by Maj. Takayasu Seno that was well known for its smart operations, left Bahilang. Before departing, Commander Seno warned all his troops: "This is a war against the youth party. Attack them resolutely. The enemy, however, is only the radical youth party. Never injure any other inhabitants. Anyone damaging the name of our glorious Imperial Guard Regiment will be strictly punished."

After closing off the four exits to the city with small groups of troops, the main force rushed into the town from the south with two tanks at its head. Field cannons were not used in this attack because the soldiers did not want to injure the general public. The youths of Pesindo resisted at the entrance with fierce firing, but the tanks opened the way, crushing the barricades, and soldiers followed behind on foot. The youths were surprised as the Japanese soldiers' bullets, which had never before been directed against Indonesians, began to hit them. They retreated, gathering in their headquarters in the central square. They shot from all windows with rifles and machine guns, but ran out when the tank guns hit the house. The battalion thus occupied the house in a short period of time. The street fighting continued until late in the day and several Japanese soldiers were killed or wounded. Since the troops closing the road to Medan at the Padang Bridge initially concealed themselves behind the west bank, a large group of the radicals who tried to run out across the bridge became victims of the machine guns from a Japanese ambush.

The next day, with the cooperation of Indonesian policemen and moderate inhabitants, the occupying force searched the entire city and arrested the hidden radical youths and agitators. Those arrested were examined again and anyone proved to be a friend of the Japanese was released. Parapat, the Tebing Branch leader of the Fifth Corps, was one of those released.

Some fifty remaining radicals were later killed and buried in a corner of the central square. All the Indonesians in the city were astonished by the unexpectedly severe attitude of the Japanese army who had looked so faint-hearted after losing the war.

BATTLE IN THE SUBURBS OF TEBING TINGGI

When the Japanese attack became known in the various estates and villages around Tebing City, the youths there did not fear the Japanese because they only had memories of their spiritless attitude after the war. So the young Indonesians came out with hunting guns from the estate office, rifles from the police box, and native spears and mountain knives, crying, "Don't be afraid of the Japanese. Let us take back Tebing City."

Battles between veterans and amateurs continued throughout the day of December 15. The Japanese army was very experienced in field battles, and the group of farmers who were amateur fighters were no match for them. Although the attackers were very brave, they were easily swept aside by Japanese rifles and machine guns.

A fight across the Padang River was particularly serious because more than a thousand Indonesians from the Sungai Rampah area rushed in. The Japanese troops waiting on the east side of the bank poured bullets on the attackers rushing across the river. The river was thus stained red with the numerous bodies floating in it.

In the afternoon, an Indonesian reported that many youths gathering in Sungai Rampah were preparing for another attack on Tebing in several trucks. Maj. Seno's battalion advanced there and swept away all the youths. The battalion advanced further to Bedagai to rescue the air force troops who they had heard were besieged there by the Indonesians. The troop of twenty soldiers had already returned to Medan, however, breaking through the siege. The Indonesian youths occupying the barracks counterattacked with rifles but eventually ran away leaving behind several bodies.

The battles around Tebing on this day were so serious that three were killed and several wounded on the Japanese side. There was no means to count the killed and wounded Indonesians.

While these battles were going on, I was waiting for the Indonesian delegates at Resident Hafas' place in Medan to go to settle the situation in Tebing. Since the situation was still very dangerous, it was only natural that the delegates were unwilling to go.

CHAPTER TEN
THE GREAT NATIONAL MORAL IMPERATIVE

SOLDIERS BURNING WITH ANGER

On December 16, all the Indonesian youths in the estates and villages around Tebing Tinggi were petrified and astonished at the ferocity of the sweeping Japanese force. All remaining youths ran far away from the villages. It was under such circumstances that I arrived from Medan with the Indonesian delegates to arbitrate the situation.

After hearing the whole story from Maj. Seno and his staff at the occupying battalion headquarters, I brought the mission to the regiment commander's residence in Bahilang Estate to meet Maj. Gen. Sawamura and try to negotiate a peace. The meeting was, however, far from conciliatory. Maj. Gen. Sawamura, looking at the mission delegates, declared that the outrages carried out by the frenzied Indonesian youths had pushed him beyond the limits of his patience. The Indonesian delegates felt threatened by the extraordinarily angry attitude of Gen. Sawamura. They were informed for the first time of the cruelty committed by the youths of their race, and were simply too astonished and terrified to say anything. I could do nothing but return with them to Tebing.

When we returned to the occupying battalion's headquarters, the battalion commander, Maj. Seno, was just hearing the reports from the search parties who were returning one after another:

Lt. so and so and eight soldiers searched such and such village and have just returned. We found the bodies of three friends buried in a farm. While we were there, two Indonesians ran away on seeing us so we shot them immediately, judging them to be the murderers.

Similar reports were heard one after another. I wondered about the attitude of the soldiers towards the residents when they found the bodies of their comrades murdered so cruelly. What could be done when those with superior arms were burning with the anger to retaliate? I did not think their anger unreasonable. However, retaliation can never be fair. How terrified would the residents be when faced with indiscriminate retaliation by soldiers speaking a foreign language? The Indonesian delegates sitting in the room with me were vacantly watching those reporting through the glass window. What would they feel if they could understand the content of the reports? I trembled, afraid that some of them might understand. They were, however, sitting in complete silence, seemingly without comprehension.

STANDING AT A CROSSROAD OF DOOM

Night fell. The Indonesian delegates silently retired to their lodgings. There was no hope at all of a solution. Although they knew of the cruelty by the Indonesian youths, they would not be bold enough to tell it as it was to the Indonesian media. Consequently, the Indonesian public in other areas would have no chance of knowing the truth. Although the Japanese soldiers believed their retaliation was reasonable, it would be reported to other Indonesians as nothing more than the one-sided cruelty of the Japanese. If the delegates were allowed to return to Medan like that, the hostility between the Indonesians and the Japanese would burn more fiercely.

The flames had already been ignited in other places. The air force stationed in Tanjung Pura Air Base was reported to be facing attack by Indonesian youths. The situation would become even more serious if the riots were to spread to all of Sumatra. In Aceh, in particular, a small group of Japanese troops were isolated and surrounded, with some of them already disarmed and being held hostage. If we failed to solve the Tebing situation, the effect would immediately spread over all Sumatra, and unarmed Japanese hostages would be threatened with massacre. At the moment, the Indonesians were astonished by the partial success of the Japanese armed operation. If we could direct this reaction correctly, we would be able to resume our place as the brothers of the Indonesians. If we mismanaged it, and it led to overall hostility, however, we would become eternal enemies. We were standing at the crossroads. If we really believed that the Japanese were the blood brothers of Indonesians, it would be necessary for us to show our love after we had shown our power.

Unfortunately, however, all the officers and soldiers who had seen the bodies of their comrades were too absorbed in their anger to analyze the political implications. Their anger was not unnatural because an army usually teaches anger against the enemy. All the soldiers seemed to share the following sentiments: "What is Indonesia? What is independence? The independence of such a cruel and insensitive people is better off destroyed."

Such feelings were burning in their angry faces. All the red and white independence flags had been taken down. People saying merdeka were struck by Japanese soldiers. Even a Japanese would be struck if he supported the Indonesians. I was perhaps the only exception because I had often been invited by this regiment to supervise the construction of the telephone system and was well respected by the soldiers of the regiment. The propaganda squad had already driven around in a car with a loud speaker announcing:

> The independence movement is no longer permitted. As was said in the Joint Decree, the Japanese army now directly governs this area. The independent Indonesian government is no longer recognized.

"What a thoughtless announcement," I thought. Indonesians and Japanese have been important comrades who fought together as Asian blood brothers. Although we were not permitted to assist independence because of our surrender, we did not have to suppress it. How sad is the careless shift to the opposing side just because of a single incident! The 5th Regiment is conforming exactly to the strategy planned by NICA or the Communists."

WE SHOULD NEVER BE AGAINST INDEPENDENCE

Desperately wanting to stop the propaganda prohibiting the independence movement, I tried negotiating with the battalion commander, but he responded: "The Japanese army is responsible for continuing the military administration under the orders of the Allied Forces. Do you want to recognize the arbitrary formation of the Indonesian government?"

Surprised, I thought to myself that I would not say it was unreasonable for the soldiers of the 5th Regiment, whose comrades were killed, to be so angry. However, what would be the result if, blind with rage, we were to challenge the independence movement? During the Japanese occupation, the desire for independence had become common among all Indonesians. It was now a kind of faith that was streaming hotly through their blood. What would happen if we declared "We are the enemy of independence"? Even if they partly or even temporarily caved in out of fear, the hostility of the Indonesian nation as a whole would never be wiped from the name of the Japanese.

If, at this moment when the position of the Japanese had become somewhat stronger, we were impelled by anger to destroy the independence movement that we ourselves had encouraged, the reputation of our Japanese nation would be completely ruined. If we were to say that we could not help it because of our anger, then we could not claim our right to condemn the Indonesians. This would be too shameful for the Japanese. Even the Allied Forces are saying only "Do not assist independence," not daring to say to destroy the movement, though they might wish it. They are an army of civilized nations who know international law. Why should we Japanese destroy Indonesian independence, especially if there is no order?

The Japanese were the ones who had planted the seed and raised the independence movement. Before the Japanese occupation, there was, in reality, little concept of Indonesia as one nation, because many races or tribes were struggling with each other under the divide-and-rule policy of the colonial government. Although a limited number of political leaders were pushing for independence, the general Indonesian public were content to be ruled by the superior foreign race, never thinking that with independence they could be equal.

When the Japanese, who are the same Mongoloids as Indonesians, kicked the Dutch out, the Indonesian public began for the first time to demand independence and equality. When the Japanese strongly urged the unity of all Indonesian races in supporting such political leaders as Sukarno and Hatta, and promoted a common Indonesian language over the many dialects as well as the national song of Indonesia Raya, the people began, for the first time, to become united as one nation. The independence movement now burning is the result of that. To abide by the regulations of the Allied Forces, we must refrain from openly assisting the independence movement. However, it is a moral imperative for us to continue to be sympathetic to independence as the brothers of Indonesians.

When we advanced south, holding high the flag of Asian liberation, they enthusiastically welcomed and cooperated with us. It would be too shameful if we were to become their enemy immediately after losing the war. History lasts forever. Looking into the distant future, we must keep our national morals intact, regardless of the very hard current situation. Maintaining our national morals is in the interests of our descendants too.

Of course we should not help Indonesian independence. But at least we should give them gentle words to soothe their fear and hostility, such as, "The Japanese army will maintain a position of neutrality towards your independence. Regrettably, we cannot help your independence, but we have no desire to disturb it. Your independence movement will not be obstructed unless you endanger the lives of Japanese. Do not be afraid of us. We are blood brothers."

We had to stop retaliation as soon as possible. Otherwise the results would be disastrous.

Maj. Gen. Shunpo Sawamura

After considering the situation this way, I took a car by myself, because it was very late and the driver was already in bed, to visit the regiment commander, Sawamura. The wet road in the rubber estate had many muddy spots due to some rain falling a short time ago. The regiment commander's residence that I had visited this afternoon was now completely quiet, like a gigantic black block in the darkness of the rubber forest. It was a wooden building that had previously been used as the residence of the estate manager, and the floor was about two meters off the ground, probably because the earth here could get so wet. At the top of the front stairs was a wide veranda with a wooden floor. In the center of the veranda was a simple wooden table, over which a bare electric light was shining faintly. In response to my call, Maj. Gen. Sawamura came out immediately and sat across the table from me. Sawamura, who was always kind to his soldiers, ordered his orderly to retire to bed and so there was no-one other than Gen. Sawamura and myself. Looking straight at him without flinching, I desperately tried to persuade him to protect our national morals for the future, as I have described above.

His Excellency, Sawamura, was completely silent. For nearly an hour he listened to me, a man more than twenty years younger than him, in complete silence. From before, I had respected him greatly and he had relied heavily on me also. He was a sincere listener. He was not a man who would depart from justice because of rank, power, or to save face. He was reputed by the Japanese civilians also to be an unusually understanding general. It was clear that he felt an unrepressable anger over the tragic death of his subordinates. He had probably no other alternative than to inflict a serious blow against the crazy youths in order to stop their pathological frenzy. In his heart, however, a calm thoughtfulness was replacing the anger. The frightful anger that he showed this afternoon to the Indonesian delegates had completely disappeared from his face. He listened in complete silence to the long lecture from me, a younger officer of much lower rank. Finally, he responded, nodding deeply, "You are right. I agree with you completely. Please do as you said."

What a splendid conversion it was! What a wonderful resolution. That was all he said. He smiled at me, pouring all his goodwill and trust upon me. I could not prevent my eyes from flooding with hot tears. I could only say one word -- "Thank you."

The midnight meeting had proved a wonderful success. Taking the wheel of my car in very high spirits, I returned to Tebing Tinggi.

NICA's STRATEGY Is RESPONSIBLE FOR EVERYTHING

The next day, December 17, dawned. Once Maj. Gen. Sawamura, respected as their father by all members of the regiment, gave the order, no-one was willing to oppose it. The commander of the occupying battalion, Maj. Seno, proclaimed the new policy, calling all officers to his headquarters. The Japanese retaliation was over at last. I asked the Indonesian delegates to hold a public meeting in the square in front of the Tebing government building. Some 2,000 citizens gathered in front of the meter-high stage placed in the center of the square.

Munar, representing the Komite Nasional Indonesia (KNI) stood on the stage first and said: "We must establish order to be independent. Our independent government is responsible for directing the people. Our Komite Nasional Indonesia mediates between the government and the people. Do not act in a thoughtless way, neglecting the direction of our government and the committee. Otherwise you may destroy your own independence."

A representative from the Partai Nasional Indonesia (PNI) stepped up next and persuaded the audience by walking around on the stage and gesturing as if he were humoring children: "The Japanese are not our enemy but our brothers. Such foolish behavior by us, the Indonesians, pleases only the Dutch. Dear comrades. Do not be deceived by the strategy of NICA, the Dutch agency. Come back, all good citizens. What should be blamed is not the independence movement but killing Japanese."

Burhan, sent by the Pesindo headquarters in Medan, spoke next, wiping his short Colman mustache: "Do not do bad things in the name of Pesindo. I am so embarrassed by being told everywhere, "Pesindo did this," "Pesindo did this." Our Medan headquarters have never given any such orders. Comrades, it was the agitation of NICA."

I thought this explanation a little strange. The night before the incident, the engineering regiment in the Rambutan Estate had intercepted the following telephone conversation between Tebing and Medan:

> "We are planning to attack the Japanese army in Tebing Tinggi tomorrow evening. Please send reinforcements from Medan."

"I see, but our party in Medan is also tied up by all that is happening. Please collect as many comrades as possible from the neighboring villages."

Although the speakers were not known, the Medan headquarters of Pesindo could not have been unaware of the conversation. I thought that Burhan was playing innocent. But I kept silent because no trouble could be expected from his position. The audience listened with their eyes wide open, surprised by the cleverness of NICA's strategy, and murmured to themselves, "Oh my goodness. It was the NICA's strategy."

The Tebing district controller of independent Indonesia, Siregar, and the East Sumatra Resident, Tengku Hafas, then gave formal addresses.

THERE Is No CHANGE IN OUR LOVE FOR INDONESIANS

As the final speaker, I got up on stage:

We Japanese are the brothers of you Indonesians. We, therefore, did not shoot Indonesians because we did not like to kill our brothers. We shot only into the sky when we were forced to defend ourselves. Unappreciative of such a stance, you Indonesians gradually became arrogant and finally killed sixty Japanese soldiers with terrible cruelty. Beyond the limits of patience, the Japanese army reluctantly retaliated against the radical youths. This was how all this started.

The Japanese army has surrendered to the Allied Forces. We are strictly prohibited from assisting Indonesian independence or giving arms to you. We, therefore, cannot directly assist your independence movement. However, neither do we have any desire to attack your quest for independence. Of course, the Dutch may wish to have the Japanese attack Indonesian independence.
However, because international law prohibits the use of those who have surrendered for military purposes, their wishes cannot be made orders. We are, therefore, keeping neutral with regard to Indonesian independence. But, our love for you Indonesian people, as our blood-brothers, will never change. Our operation at this time was an unavoidable counterattack, because we were being murdered by our beloved brothers. Once Indonesians stop killing us, we will no

longer attack our brothers. We simply scold our younger brother for his behavior. This does not mean that our love has changed. You, good citizens, have no need for any more fear. Please return to your homes and work.

Who would be pleased by such a foolish struggle between brothers? We Japanese do not want to fight again now that the war is over. Our only concern is to send our soldiers safely back to their parents' homes in our motherland. We cannot be patient, however, if the lives of important soldiers are endangered. If you anger the Japanese, the sacrifice will also be on your side. If you were to repeat such actions, in which direction would your independence movement go? Neither the Japanese nor the Indonesians are pleased. Who would be pleased by such an incident? [I did not say the Dutch would be pleased, because I would be accused of war crimes if I said that.]

We all are Asian brothers. The Chinese are also our brothers. You should not perscute the Chinese. Do not struggle with your brothers in Asia.

The 2,000 members of the audience listened, nodding deeply, without even laughing at my poor Indonesian.

INDONESIANS, Do NOT BE DISCOURAGED

A happy look began to appear on the faces of the audience for the first time. When I stepped down from the stage, the delegates of the various Indonesian parties came to me one after another and shook my hand, their faces beaming with delight. I felt an uncontrollable desire to encourage them aloud: "Dear Indonesian youths. Do not be discouraged. Go on mustering your courage for the independence struggle."

But I had to keep quiet, because I would be accused of a war crime. What I wanted to say, however, was already being shouted by several of the Indonesian delegates. In a cheerful voice they shouted out the call of independence to the public who were watching our faces rather nervously, "Merdeka!"

The public, who had been frightened by the menace of the Japanese soldiers, were watching in disbelief the look on my face, the face of a Japanese officer, as I smiled at the Indonesian delegates as they cried,

"Merdeka!" They initially kept quiet, but gradually began to respond in low voices, "Merdeka."

The delegates of the mission unanimously blamed NICA when they saw the public hesitate in responding to their independence call. Hearing their denunciation of NICA with a somewhat strange feeling, I began to prepare to depart with the delegates. It might be true that NICA had done something. However, the Japanese, whose clumsy military administration had given the pretext for the NICA strategy, and the Indonesians, who were easily deceived by such a strategy, must also reflect on their own foolishness.

No-one seemed to be thinking of the Communist strategy. In reality, there were no radical Communists among the local population, because the Communist party in East Sumatra was indepenent from Java and Moscow. But insurgents from Java quite possibly might have been there. Among the people captured by the battalion, there were several strangers from Java whose purpose for being there was unknown. The sudden change in the tone of the press and public opinion might have been influenced by the insurgents. The youth party in Tebing might have been unwittingly manipulated by the agitation of underground Communists, as in Central Java. The real truth may never be known.

THANKING A FORMER HEIHO

On our way to Medan, we once again dropped in at the village of Sungai Rampah. In response to a call from the director of general affairs, Tengku Damrah, a group of villagers fearfully came out and gathered in the village square. Beginning with Tengku Hafas (the East Sumatra Resident), the delegates spoke in turn to the villagers.

> The Japanese will not harm you unless you harm them. Please return to work; you have nothing to worry about. The Tebing incident occurred because the youths who were agitated by the strategy of NICA harmed the Japanese. Do not cause any trouble with the Japanese. The Japanese army has no desire to disturb our independence movement. We must continue our movement without being discouraged.

While they were speaking, I looked around the faces of the audience, one by one, because of a story I had heard. Several days ago, a Japanese group headed by Maj. Takeuchi was captured by Indonesian youths in this village and confined in a prison to the southwest after being robbed of their car, weapons, and personal effects. When they were about to be killed, a youth persuaded the leaders to stop the murders and then secretly treated the prisoners kindly, bringing them food. When questioned, he told them that he had been educated by Capt. Fusayama as a Heiho with the Imperial Guard Division's communications troops in Medan and talked fondly about his life at that time. As a result, I wanted to find him and thank him.

Because I could not find any face that I recognized, I told the village headman the story and asked him to find him. An old man ran into the village and immediately brought back a youth. It was Maladdin. Although he wore a regular farmer's clothes instead of a uniform, I could easily identify him as Maladdin whom I had previously taught. "I heard that you were so kind to Maj. Takeuchi and the other Japanese soldiers that you saved their lives. Thank you very much."

Thanking him, I extended my hand but he saluted tensely in the Indonesian manner, touching my hand tip with his hand and then bending his body with his hand on his chest. He was the most outstanding Heiho that I had taught, with a smart brain and a strong body. After the war's end he returned to his home village and joined the youth party, Pesindo, but he could not become a leader because he was from a low-class family. When the youths had wanted to kill the captured Japanese, including Maj. Takeuchi, he stopped them by stressing the possible repercussions: "This is a Japanese colonel. If we were to kill such a high-ranking officer, the Japanese army would definitely retaliate in anger. We should not kill them."

Seeing a Japanese officer talking in a friendly way and thanking Maladdin, the people of the village opened their eyes wide in admiration and envy.

Meanwhile Chinese merchants also came out of their roadside stores. Seen off by a great number of people, we left Sungai Rampah and then stopped off in Bedagai, another place where there had been riots. This was the place where the twenty airforce troops were besieged by Indonesian youths. When the Japanese troops from Tebing attacked the youths, Raja Bedagai (chief of the Bedagai kingdom) was killed while caught up in the battle. The wife of the the Raja clung to me crying and appealed to me in tears, "My husband approached the youths in order to stop them fighting. Nevertheless, the Japanese army shot him dead together with the youths."

Although I sympathized deeply with her, I could not do anything. Resident Tengku Hafas, whose wife was a sister of the killed Raja, tried to explain with teary eyes. However they might explain it, I could not find any words to speak. It was indeed a battle. When two parties are shooting at each other, risking their lives, distinguishing details from far away is impossible. I expressed my sincere sympathy by nodding but could say nothing. We thus made our way to Medan.

MY POSITION Is VERY DELICATE

On arriving in Medan, I immediately started thinking about the newspapers. As the mission was being disbanded, I said to Resident Hafas, "One of the significant factors worsening the situation was the irresponsible reporting by the newspapers. The reality that you personally encountered in Tebing was much different from the reports in the newspapers that you read in Medan, wasn't it? I wonder why the newspapers like so much to estrange the Indonesians from the Japanese by reporting lies. Your government is responsible for directing public opinion. Hereafter, please strictly censor the papers beforehand so as not to permit the delivery of irresponsible reports."

Resident Hafas was, however, still afraid of the newspapers. He was a nervous aristocrat, with the weakness of the propertied class. He was afraid of being attacked by the newspapers if he carelessly approached them. I pleaded from my heart, "Don't worry. This is your chance. It would be good for the government to exert control over the journalists in this instance."

When I spoke in this way, Tengku Damrah, the director of general affairs, who was a well-experienced, thoughtful man, extended some advice: "Tuan, advance censorship is not easy to carry out. The newspapers are writing independently. It is impossible for our government to control them directly. We can guide them as much as possible. We will warn them if their descriptions are wrong, and instruct them to write correctly. We will give them the true information about the Tebing incident and instruct them to report the truth. Tuan, is that all right with you?"

Feeling that his opinion was reasonable, I answered, "All right, I understand. Please do it that way." I understood that advance censorship was impossible. If advance censorship was mandatory, the newspapers, for whom speed is all important, would lose their lives. In addition, the current government did not seem to have the ability to establish the function of daily censorship. I agreed with Damrah, after reconsidering.

The Tebing incident was reported in a big way in the newspapers the next day. A Eurasian typist working in our liaison office, Agnes, excitedly showed us the paper, "Your name is in the paper!"

I intentionally pretended not to be concerned, but it was not an unpleasant feeling in my heart. However, I was still not permitted to enjoy things easily. I was actually in a dangerous position. I knew that. If the Indonesian newspapers exaggerated my good will towards Indonesian independence, I would soon be arrested by the Dutch as a war criminal for assisting the independence movement. On the other hand, if the papers were to report that I was undermining independence, even a little, I would be exposed to the danger of assassination by Indonesian youths.

I fully realized the difficulty of my current political position. Appearing in the newspapers was somehow dangerous.

THE BATTLE ON BALI STREET

My comrades in the liaison office told me a very interesting story when I returned from Tebing. While I was busily occupied by matters surrounding the Tebing incident, another big incident had occurred in Medan. It was on the afternoon of December 15, just as I was waiting in vain for the Indonesian delegates to arrive at the residence of Resident Hafas. We thought at that time that the Indonesian-Japanese conflict in Tebing must have pleased the Allied Forces, particularly the Dutch, who hoped that Indonesian hostilities would be focused on the Japanese. However, hostility toward the Dutch, it seemed, had not been reduced.

The incident happened on a section of Bali Street. As in the incident in Pematang Siantar, the instigator was again an Ambonese soldier. The soldier wrested the red and white badge of independence from the breast of an Indonesian child and trampled it under his feet on the asphalt pavement. The angry people around them immediately rushed upon the soldier. The astonished Ambonese fired his automatic gun as a threat and ran into a nearby clubhouse that was for the amusement of Dutch soldiers.

The sound of gunfire roared throughout the area. Groups came from all directions and began to throw stones.

The Dutch soldiers who were enjoying themselves in the clubhouse took their weapons and began shooting from the windows. Meanwhile, Indonesians also began to shoot with a few rifles, and some threw hand grenades. Half-naked Dutch officers shot pistols from the upstairs windows and Eurasian women screamed inside.

Informed of this emergency, TKR troops ran to the place and began to attack. An officer of the TKR was shouting commands in Japanese. Many bottle grenades were being thrown.

The place was only a few hundred meters from the Japanese liaison office in Lombok Avenue. The Japanese in the office were afraid that, if they were to remain mere spectators, they would surely be accused of war crimes like Lt. Col. Muromoto in the Pematang Siantar incident. Consequently, Lt. Honda, who used to teach the Giyugun (Indonesian Volunteer Army), hastened to the place and rushed in front of the attackers spreading his arms wide and shouting for them to stop. The soldiers from the TKR who had been trained by him stopped, and the battle was barely controlled. This incident was the first big conflict between the Indonesians and the Dutch in Medan. (There is now a monument in this place commemorating the incident.) The Japanese in the liaison office were deeply moved by the loyalty of the members of the TKR to their former teacher. At the same time, they were deeply afraid that the presence of a Japanese might have been seen as an attempt to undermine the independence struggle.

CHAPTER ELEVEN
JAPANESE-INDONESIAN FRIENDSHIP IS RESTORED

CLEAR SKIES AFTER A TYPHOON

The newspapers in Medan were again becoming cooperative towards the Japanese. Since our office had an interpreter who had studied Indonesian at a foreign language college, I left the newspaper briefings to him. The tone of the newspapers became better day by day. People were talking in the street as follows:

> The Japanese are not our enemy. A struggle with the Japanese is disadvantageous to us. Challenging the Japanese army will only invite a bitter response. Don't make the Japanese our enemy by being deceived by NICA's strategy.

This conclusion spread rapidly over the whole of Sumatra.

Because the radical youths who had behaved recklessly, neglecting the instructions from the Indonesian government, had been dealt a heavy blow in the Tebing incident, the authority of the independent government was somewhat established. Indonesian policemen recovered enough power to at least arrest thieves. The Indonesian government gradually strengthened its voice and began efforts to unify and streamline the independence movement.

I visited many places to warn Japanese people not to do wrong and encouraged them to converse with Indonesians to understand their desires and their conditions. The area of Pangkalan Brandan also became quiet. The youths who had attacked and burned the Tanjung Pura Air Base became calm again. The position of the Japanese, which had sunk to an extreme low, rose day by day and the Indonesians began to respect the Japanese again.

On the other side, the soldiers of the 5th Regiment in Tebing, who had been so angry on seeing the bodies of their murdered comrades, also recovered their composure. The propaganda officer of the occupying battalion seriously regretted his announcement by loudspeaker that, "The independence movement in Indonesia is no longer permitted." He often visited me in the liaison office and stressed, "It was not my true intention."

In order to prevent a recurrence of the conflict between the Japanese and the Indonesians, I agreed to meet periodically with Governor Teuku Hasan at his private residence to communicate the mutual claims of the Japanese and Indonesians.

ROBBERY BY JAPANESE SOLDIERS

When the Indonesians were calm again, undesirables among the Japanese began to appear. One day, when I visited Governor Hasan for our regular meeting, he issued a serious protest to me with a very sour face. According to him, a small squad of Japanese in the Pangkalan Brandan area had roamed through the neighboring villages and stolen gold necklaces, earrings, and bracelets from an Indonesian woman in her home. A similar robbery was repeated twice in the same area. Governor Hasan added:

> A variety of people can be found even in the Japanese army. Consequently, I do not intend to criticize the whole army for this single case. But if such cases are allowed to continue, your side must be responsible for the public hostility toward the Japanese that will occur. It is very regrettable that such an action occurred on the Japanese side when you and I are making such efforts to improve Japanese-Indonesian relations.

I retired feeling extremely ashamed. What heartless men they were! The Japanese had often called the Indonesians rioters, and blamed massacres and pillage on the Indonesians. Nevertheless, the Japanese themselves were doing these wrong things once their position had become stronger. Men like that, who are cowardly when placed in a weak position, usually dare do wrong against the weaker side when their own position becomes stronger. The way to establish a just peace is not to enforce justice only on the weak or defeated. A real just peace can be established only when the strong or the victors enforce justice on themselves. Because the Indonesians were afraid of the Japanese at this moment, it is the very time when we should be just and try to recover the Indonesians' trust.

ARE YOU REALLY A JAPANESE?

The Japanese garrison in the area of Pangkalan Brandan was an air defense regiment directly controlled by the 25th Army headquarters and so it was not a part of our Imperial Guard Division. However, I could not ignore the incident because the Indonesians saw all Japanese forces as the same Japanese army. As soon as I returned to the liaison office, I telephoned the headquarters of the air defense regiment and conveyed the protest from Governor Hasan to the adjutant. And so as not to sound too harsh, I added: "I do not necessarily believe that the report from the Indonesians was entirely accurate. But, if such a thing did happen, it is very embarrassing. I am sorry to bother you, but I ask that you sincerely look into it."

The answer from the other end was, however, a very cold one that I never expected, "Such a thing could never happen in our regiment." I was very surprised and responded, "How can you know without investigating it?"

"Our regiment is well-disciplined under the excellent leadership of our commander. Such a thing could never happen to our honorable troops. There is no need to look into it. Tell that to the governor, as he is called by the natives."

His answer was extremely curt and impolite. I questioned him further with disgust: "Why don't you want to examine it? Among any troops, who can guarantee that no single person makes a mistake? Anyway, the protest clearly indicated the time and place. You know? There is no smoke without fire. There must be something. How can you deny it without investigating? A serious misunderstanding could result from such an absurd attitude."

The adjutant invented a pretext from these last words. He protested fiercely, "What? What is absurd? Are you saying that our regiment is absurd? I cannot let such a word pass."

At that moment, a sharp impact sounded over the telephone and then the thick voice of an elderly person said arrogantly, "Who are you? What is your rank?"

He seemed to be someone of high rank. Straightening myself out of a habit acquired during my army service, I answered his question with some trepidation, "Yes Sir. I am Captain Fusayama managing Indonesian affairs at the liaison office. May I ask your name?"

"I am the regiment commander. Are you criticizing my regiment? Of what importance are Indonesians? Why do you respect the natives so much? You must be manipulated by the Indonesians. You foolish person! This is why the Japanese army is not appreciated by the Indonesians. Are you really a Japanese?"

What violent language! How offensive it was to me, as a Japanese, as well as to our Indonesian brothers! It was a definite indication of an unusual military person who was intending to display an outrageous sense of distorted pride and egoism. It was surprising that he had not yet been released from such delusions even after the unconditional surrender. His subordinates were like they were because their commander was that way. Though I flinched for a moment because of the difference in rank, I became inflamed with anger. I refuted him, "Why do you ask if I am Japanese? All of this is for the honor of the Japanese. Obtaining the trust of the inhabitants is for the sake of the Japanese, isn't it? What an insult your question is, asking if I am Japanese!"

While stammering this out, I had a good idea and continued without giving him time to argue: "All right. If you want to be this way, I will report this to army headquarters. I am carrying out my duties according to the orders of the army commander. I cannot accomplish my duties if troops such as yours are left to behave as they did. I will ask for my instructions, after reporting everything to army headquarters."

It was a very good idea to mention the army's name. This force was afraid of army headquarters because it was directly controlled by it. A person who is unusually strong toward his juniors is always very weak before his seniors.

There was silence for a while at the other end of the telephone. Then, a very gentle voice, as if it came from a completely different person, reached me through the receiver, "Hello? I probably went too far in my talk, eh? Don't take it badly, please. We shall immediately examine the case carefully. Do not think badly of us. Hey, Adjutant, come and get the details of the case from this man and investigate it in a hurry."

It was a surprising change beyond my expectations. A regiment commander, a colonel, an elderly person with a bald head, apologized in a truckling manner. I had never experienced such a case during the entire period of my army service.

The adjutant's attitude thereafter was also extremely polite. The change in the commander's attitude after his apology did not sound insincere to me. I thought he was probably an inherently good man. The personnel customs of the military made a good man bad. This custom was defined as acting willfully to preserve the dignity of the army by hiding the misdeeds of one's subordinates. This was a traditional habit in the Japanese army. It was a deep-rooted evil that was the main cause of bringing Japan to the depths of defeat in this tragedy.

I doubted, however, that the problem was confined to soldiers. It seemed to result from the factionalism that was common to government officials, policemen, and other groups formed by the Japanese. Among them, the evil was most serious in military society because it had the greatest power. It was important that the spirit of fair play overcome personal feeling and egoism.

JAPANESE-INDONESIAN FRIENDSHIP IS RESTORED

Thereafter, this kind of trouble no longer existed. Communication between the Japanese and Indonesians was reestablished everywhere. Arms and goods from the Japanese army began secretly to reach the Indonesians behind the backs of the Allied Forces. Indonesians once again began to feel that the Japanese were their friends.

These days, the food situation of the Japanese army had improved remarkably. It was not only because vegetables were harvested again in plenty from the farms we ran for our own support. The strict rationing of our food staples by the Allied Forces had become a dead letter. Because of the independence war, the Allied Forces could not leave the area of Medan and Belawan, where they had entrenched themselves. The Japanese army stayed out of that area, together with the Indonesian inhabitants, and their good relations were restored. Because the Indonesians boycotted Dutch money and the British military currency, Japanese military currency was still the only effective currency in Indonesia. We could, therefore, purchase rice and other foods as much as we wanted, willingly supplied by the Indonesians outside the control of the Allied Forces.

Obtaining protein foods also became easy. The Japanese soldiers hunted wild boar that lived in plentiful numbers in the jungles, oil-palm estates, and even around the villages. Some troops stationed near big rivers shot gigantic snapping turtles -- nearly one meter in size -- to eat, and they were extraordinarily delicious. We could use as many bullets as we liked for hunting. Before the Tebing Tinggi incident, we could not use bullets because we had to keep all arms until they could be turned over to the Allied Forces. But after the Japanese army used some bullets in the Tebing incident, the Allied Forces welcomed their use, expecting that they would be directed against the Indonesians. We were thus free to use bullets for other purposes by explaining that we were using them to defend ourselves against Indonesian attacks. Ironically, this excuse was also used when Japanese troops passed bullets secretly to the Indonesians.

AN UNEXPECTED VICTIM

The Tebing Tinggi incident had caused a problem that was extremely embarrassing to me. In the middle of the incident, Mr. Fusali Rem, a brother-in-law of the Maharaja Soankupon Siregar, disappeared. He had lived in Surabaya from before the war and visited his birthplace in Sumatra just before the incident. While staying with his relatives in Tebing, he was arrested by a Japanese search team and did not return. Soankupon's family anxiously asked me to rescue him. I thought that this request was a good opportunity to repay Soankupon for his kindness to me and went immediately to Tebing. I was, however, to discover the worst.

When I visited the occupying battalion headquarters and made inquiries, mentioning that I was acquainted with him through Maharaja Soankupon, the battalion commander scratched his head and was frank with me:

> Captain Fusayama, I am very sorry. He was killed. As you know, our division headquarters informed us repeatedly of the warning from 16th Army headquarters that radical agitators from Java were infiltrating

Sumatra. We therefore searched the whole of Tebing Tinggi for strangers immediately after occupying it. He was captured by a search squad and discovered to have come recently from Java. Consequently, he was judged to be an agitator and killed, together with the other Indonesians responsible for the murders of Japanese. I did not know that he was a brother of your friend. I am very sorry."

Maj. Seno was a typical professional officer who had graduated from the Japanese military academy. He was a very straightforward man and well known for his excellent command abilities in battle, even though he was young. Because we had been acquainted from before, he was honest with me about the facts, not hiding anything. I could find no words as I watched his face in helpless astonishment. The reality was really the worst. I felt as if cold water had been poured on me and energy drained from my body.

When I was last here as a mediator, I had found some Indonesians with their hands tied behind their back in the next room. Mr. Fusali Rem must have been there. If I had known that at the time -- if Soankupon had told me about his brother-in-law -- I would have been able to save him. I had so many regrets, but now it was too late. I recalled that, when I looked inside that room, many terrified eyes looked back at me and a tremble ran through the room, deeply shocking me. When I imagined myself or a relative of mine in there, subject to the terror of death, an unbearable sorrow and anger filled my heart.

Standing in front of the battalion commander who had revealed all the facts to me, I was on the point of blaming him, red with anger, wanting to ask, "Why did you not carefully examine them before killing them?" But I could not say that. It was war. I, myself, had also seen the bodies of the Japanese soldiers massacred by the Indonesians. How could I blame the soldiers for their anger towards the supposed agitators who were responsible for the murder of their comrades?

Before the Tebing incident, many unarmed Japanese were massacred by Indonesians in Java. I had myself heard the repeated warning that radical agitators were infiltrating from Java to incite the massacre of Japanese here. It was, therefore, not unnatural for the soldiers of this battalion to think that Mr. Fusali Rem was an agitator when they found out had just recently come from Java.

A HEART-BREAKING LIE

However, it was hardly possible for me to tell the truth to Soankupon and Nirwan who loved me as one of their family and had cooperated in settling incidents with consistent sympathy for the Japanese. It was impossible for me to say, "Your brother, your uncle, was killed by Japanese troops commanded by my friend."

For a while, I did not know what to do and was deeply distressed. But finally I thought, the thing for me to do now is not the work of a historian who mercilessly gathers up past facts. My duty must be to take the responsibility of constructing a future relationship so as to make both Indonesians and Japanese happy. I decided that I must even lie in performing this duty.

In accordance with my request, the battalion commander gave the following fictitious explanation:

> When the Japanese rushed into Tebing city, the people who resisted or ran were killed. Many were captured, but those with no or little relation to the attack on the Japanese were released the next day. Many of the released people tried to run out of the city across the Padang bridge, and became entangled in a battle that was going on there between the Japanese and the Indonesians coming from the villages, and they were killed in the fray. Fusali Rem might have been in the crowd.

When I returned to Medan and reported the story in this way, both Soankupon and Nirwan nodded sorrowfully and said, "Thank you very much. We hope that he may still be alive somewhere, but that possibility seems small."

Regardless of my words, it seemed hard for them to believe. Some other information might also have come from relatives in Tebing. So Maharaja Soankupon asked me repeatedly, "Would you please investigate once more?"

I was obliged to visit the battalion headquarters again and brought back once more the fictitious explanation. Feeling sorry for me as I relayed the story with some difficulty, Nirwan kindly interceded for me, saying, "Father. It is difficult to know what goes on in battle. Let us forget it."

I could not help, however, suffering from a heartbreaking grief, even more so after those kind words. Even after that, though all the family members always welcomed me with an unchanged warmth, I did not know if they were really convinced by my explanation.

JAPANESE DESERTERS FIGHT BRAVELY

The conflict between Indonesians and Japanese was now completely over. However, Indonesian guerrilla attacks against the Allied Forces were increasing in scale and frequency. I enjoyed visiting the intelligence unit of the Fifth Corps (Pasukan Kelima) in the evening to hear the inside story after I read of a guerrilla attack in a newspaper.

The day after a conflict occurred close to the city hospital in Medan, Ismed told me the following story:

> The battle yesterday was really tremendous. In the morning, a search team from the British army came to the village of Kebun Pisang on the eastern side of Serdang Street. Since the British-Indian troops were often ambushed by Indonesian guerrillas around there, they examined all the houses and captured ten innocent people who happened to be there. The squad killed the ten immediately, buried the bodies, and left. While we were angrily searching the place, a British truck driven by Indian soldiers happened to pass by. We rushed and surrounded the truck. An Indian soldier jumped down and fired his automatic gun, rotating it at random. As soon as one whole round of bullets was spent, one of our comrades lying on the ground stood up, drawing out a Japanese sword tied to his back, and dexterously stabbed the Indian soldier. The other soldiers ran away terrified, and we Indonesians captured one military truck.
>
> Expecting that the British army would come to retaliate, many Indonesians gathered there and waited in hiding. Just as expected, a British-Indian unit came to attack with an armored car at their head. The Indonesians who were waiting there in high spirits, threw hand grenades one after another against the armored car, but none exploded because in the confusion they forgot to ignite them. I think you know the mosque with a red brick wall just to the east of the city hospital. A Japanese deserter was in the mosque commanding a group of Indonesians. Indignantly he picked up a grenade himself,

carefully ignited it, and threw it with a good aim. The grenade fell right on the car and exploded with a terrific noise. The car stalled and the driver's seat was destroyed. The Japanese soldier was splendid. The astonished British-Indian soldiers hastily retreated, and the battle turned to an exchange of shots from a distance. The British antitank guns perforated the brick wall of the mosque like a beehive, and then the whole building fell down. But, by this time, the Japanese deserter had already beaten a hasty retreat.

By looking straight through Serdang Street from our liaison office at the north end of Lombok Avenue we could see this mosque. Consequently, as unconcerned spectators we could observe the antitank guns firing from their side of the street.

Later, one evening the intelligence unit youths told me another story:

Last night we attacked the barracks of the Dutch army in Herbetia. It had been a Dutch barracks since before the war. We rushed into the barracks, pushing down the wooden defense wall and inflicted heavy casualties. Unfortunately, however, the two Japanese deserters who had led our attack were killed. They had rushed at the head of the group and stabbed many enemies with their Japanese swords drawn from the sheaths tied behind their backs, but they were finally killed by shots from the Ambonese soldiers. We very much regret that their bodies were seized by the enemy.

How sorrowful their sacrifice was! When the Japanese army surrendered and was prohibited from assisting Indonesian independence, many Japanese soldiers, from a variety of motives, deserted to join the Indonesian independence war. Some deserted after losing hope in their own future when they received reports that all their relatives had been killed in the air-raid bombing of Japan. Some deserted, despondent at their motherland being occupied by the enemy. Most people connected with the military police or special services deserted when the Allied Forces began to search for war criminals, because it was rumored that all of them would be accused. There were also some deserters attracted by native lovers. A common motivation for all, however, was to carry out the national promise to liberate Indonesians which had not been fulfilled by the Japanese nation because the war had been lost.

Rebuilt Mosque at the End of Serdang Street

British Officers' Houses on Serdang Street

Hearing from the Indonesian youths the stories of Japanese deserters, I could hardly restrain my tears. They had fought bravely, but their deaths seemed so pitiful to me.

THE GUERRILLAS' HOLIDAY

I was also told a strange story:

> Last night, we attacked the barracks of the British army at the northeast end of town. We approached the barracks by crawling through a farm. It was really thrilling when we threw hand grenades into the yard. Surprised by the sudden explosion, the British, in consternation, began to shoot at random. No bullets could hit us because we were lying close to the earth as we had been taught by the Japanese army. We, the members of the Fifth Corps, were the bravest. My only trouble, however, was that my only pair of trousers got very muddy crawling through the farm. Because it is rainy today, there will be no guerrilla attack tonight. If we crawl through the muddy farm after rain, it will be awfully difficult to clean our clothes.

Jusuf told us this story. In warm Sumatra, the youths usually wore shirts without jackets and Jusuf always had a white shirt. But his shirt was never white enough, probably because he lived alone and was not good at laundry. His story sounded very curious to me because, for a Japanese, it was common sense that a rainy day provided the best opportunity for a surprise guerrilla attack.

It was a curious war, too, because they were talking then about their guerrilla exploits with laughter, and planning the next guerrilla attack at the corner of Lombok Street, less than 100 meters from the British barracks they had attacked the previous night. In addition, the person listening to them was a Japanese officer who had surrendered to the British.

JAPANESE DESERTERS WITH WHITE-CLOTH BANDS

Japanese deserters were fighting bravely in many places. One day, Nirwan told me the following story which he had heard from his cousin:

> I have a cousin in Pesindo, Imbalo; I think you know him. He told

me a story of some wonderful Japanese deserters. Four Japanese soldiers were in the attacking force. They had Japanese swords on their backs. With each of them holding a rifle, they approached the British barracks in front of the Indonesian troops. I think you know the line of two-story houses on the north side of Serdang Street. We attacked the place. The whole British barracks were very quiet with everyone asleep. Only the officers' house was lit brightly, and a few officers were still working under a lamp.

After preparing for the attack by furnishing the Indonesians with rifles and machine guns around the barracks, the four Japanese stole into the yard alone. One of them stood up in the shade of some plants and skilfully shot out the light in the officers' room. The inside of the house became instantly dark and the outside was lit faintly by the moon. The four Japanese stood up simultaneously and shot down the British officers running out in surprise. What a glorious scene it was! They looked really heroic. They wore a white-cloth band across their backs -- the sign of a suicide attacker. Holding his rifle at the ready in the distance, my cousin clearly saw the British officers falling with a groan under the Japanese swords which glittered in the moonlight.

The British were reinforced from other barracks, and both sides then exchanged shots. The Japanese hastily retreated away from the barracks, but one of them fell inside the grounds, after being shot on the lawn. No Indonesian was brave enough to go in to rescue him. Two Japanese silently crawled back into the garden under the crossfire of bullets and, with all their effort, succeeded in pulling their wounded friend out. But his body had been pierced by nine bullets and he was seriously injured. He was brought to the city hospital and the division commander of the TKR, Col. Tahir, visited him the next day to express his appreciation for his bravery. However, he died yesterday, sadly mourned by all his war comrades.

Holding my breath, I listened to the story. The Japanese deserters were fighting bravely, but tragically. If his parents or brothers were still alive somewhere in his home country, with what a lament would they hear this news? We should, however, appreciate that they were helping the Indonesians on behalf of the Japanese nation, which by losing the war, failed to carry out its promise to liberate Indonesia. I thanked them with all my heart, on behalf of the Japanese nation. Some 1,700 Japanese deserters in all of Indonesia (there were 500 in Sumatra) had joined the independence war, and the majority of them were killed in battle.

INDIAN SOLDIERS CHANGING SIDES

A battalion of the Indonesian volunteer army was actively fighting at the airport, to the south of Medan. Their head was Nip Xarim, a son of Abdul Xarim. When the Japanese army began to march south in 1941, Nip Xarim's father had been arrested as an independence leader by the Dutch and he himself escaped to Singapore. When the special service agency of the Japanese army, the Fujiwara agency, occupied Penang and began to broadcast propaganda from the Penang radio station, Nip Xarim joined the agency as an announcer, speaking English, Indonesian, and Acehnese, to call for his nation's liberation. When our Imperial Guard Division landed in Sumatra after conquering Singapore, he returned to his home in Medan and worked as a clerk for the Japanese military government.

When Japan surrendered, he organized a battalion based in the Two River Estate, 18 kilometers south of the Medan Polonia Airport. He had many excellent Indonesians on his staff and was assisted by sixteen Japanese deserters. He also had a close friend, Maj. Eiichi Itoh, in the Japanese air base battalion, from whom he secretly received many arms and war materials.

His battalion launched repeated guerrilla attacks on the British-Indian forces defending the airport and ambushed search squads coming down from the south, capturing many Indian soldiers. Because he treated them warmly, all of the captured Indian soldiers became soldiers for Nip Xarim. Although the Indian soldiers in the British-Indian army were supposed to be enemies of the Indonesians, the majority of them, particularly those who were Moslems, were very sympathetic to the Indonesian independence movement, because India was also pushing for independence. In response to the persuasion of their friends in the Two River Estate, many Indian soldiers began to desert with their arms. Embarrassed by this, the British later sent all Indian Moslem soldiers back to India.

DESERTING AMBONESE SOLDIERS

The youths of the intelligence unit told me another interesting story:

> In our corps, an Ambonese who has converted from being a Dutch spy to become a freedom fighter is fighting together with us. He had come from Australia together with the Dutch army to suppress the independence movement. But, changing his mind in the face of the earnest independence movement of his own nation, he deserted to join our group. In guerrilla attacks, the ambushing arrangements he directs are really excellent. He always stands at the front of us, sweeping the enemy with bullets from the Tommy gun that he brought with him when he deserted. We now trust him to lead a unit.

During the war, as mentioned earlier, the Allied Forces kidnapped many Indonesian youths by approaching the coast in submarines. They then educated them as spies in a school in Australia. The graduates from the spy school returned to Indonesia with the Dutch army when they landed in Sumatra. The hired Indonesian soldiers in the Dutch army, such as the Ambonese, were initially quite arrogant when they landed at Belawan port, because of the authority they borrowed from the victorious forces, and they dealt harshly with the Japanese and Indonesian people. Once they came to Medan and observed their country's independence movement, however, some of them changed their minds and deserted with their arms to join the independence struggle.

This was a serious problem for the Dutch. There was no means of knowing how many of the deserters had really changed their mind and how many were actually undermining the independence movement by assuming the guise of freedom fighters. There would also be some who were initially spies but would later change their minds. A Japanese proverb says, "Blood is thicker than water." Even the Ambonese had Indonesian blood. The time of the Dutch conquering Indonesia by using Indonesian soldiers was coming to an end.

THE FALL OF SIHITE

I questioned the youths in the intelligence unit about the recent situation of Sihite, their commander. They answered, "Sihite is increasingly busy planning and directing the guerrillas. He has no time to rest."

I said to them, "Your people are attacking the enemy carelessly and indiscriminately. You must be careful, because it would be very harmful if you were to irritate the British too much. You must be selective in fighting the enemy."

They nodded and answered, "We know that too. However, because it is often rumored that Sihite is an agent of NICA, he cannot help but intensify the guerrilla attacks to prove that he is not a NICA agent. But, then, when he increases the attacks, he is said to be intensifying troubles for the independence movement on behalf of NICA. He is trapped in a difficult dilemma."

Hearing this, I thought Sihite was nearing his end. Sihite, who had haughtily played with fate with a hidden smile, seemed to have fallen into a plight, being played with by fate.

CHAPTER TWELVE
LOVE AND HATE

TERRORISM TOWARDS THE WHITE PEOPLE

Terrorism towards Europeans and Eurasians began to occur frequently. A Danish couple who lived by Sultan Lake were suddenly murdered in their home. They had a daughter who had fallen in love with a British officer staying in Medan, and after a very quick wedding ceremony the newly weds had flown off to Bangkok from Medan airport. The girl who became the wife of an officer of the victorious army left happily, but her parents who stayed behind were cruelly murdered. In Medan every night, dreadful blades of hatred were stained with blood. Sorrowful hatred. A ghostly air was overflowing in Medan, displacing the affectionate humanity that was proper for mankind. I grieved deeply over the prevalence of terrorism.

From a long-term perspective, however, this may be considered inevitable in order for the page of history to be turned. In the past when the white people were proclaiming themselves the almighty ruler, how many Indonesian workers were whipped to death as saboteurs by the European managers? In the large estates in East Sumatra before the war, numerous so-called contract coolies (*orang kontrak*) were working. They were brought in from the overpopulated agricultural areas of Java under blind contracts after sealing with their thumbs the charters made by the slave dealers, without knowing even where they were going because they were illiterate. Although many of them died of malaria while clearing the wild forests, their places were easily filled with more slaves from Java. They were easily replaced expendables.

They slept together, huddled in a huge nipa house called a *pondok*, and were not permitted to have a home even if married. Under the contract, they worked, ate, and slept. They were domestic animals rather than human beings, and the death of some of them was nothing more than a slight financial loss to the estate manager. Such a situation was illustrated in detail in a documentary novel written by a Hungarian who spent some years as a hired estate manager in Sumatra.

According to his novel, *Coolies in Sumatra*, when a European came to work in an estate, he usually had a temporary wife called a *nyai*. He could pick up any pretty woman he liked from among the workers, regardless of whether she already had a husband or lover. The wife came into the master's bedroom in the manager's house only when called to bed by her master, and otherwise slept in the slave room on an earthen floor. No natives were considered human. Even the clerks in the estate office were not permitted to step up to the floor of the white people's residence.

The Eurasian children born to the couple were raised to a level comparable to that of the white people by being given Dutch nationality, but their mothers remained in the position of a native slave. Even in Medan, I had been very surprised to see two Eurasian teenagers abusively scolding their mother as their servant.

The Indonesians were now fighting for the life or death of their nation to free themselves from such a situation. We, therefore, could not blame only the Indonesians if some of them become crazy and cruel. Their hostility was directed against all Europeans, calling them *orang Belanda*, because the attitude of despising the natives was common to all European colonists. That is why the Danish couple were killed so cruelly.

A EURASIAN HOME IS ATTACKED AND BURNED

One night, a house in Serdang Street was burnt down. Because a fire was rare in tropical Sumatra since there are no heaters, the next day I visited the intelligence unit to inquire about the case. According to the youths, the house had been burnt by their Fifth Corps. It was the home of a Eurasian who was the director of the mechanical workers at the Medan Telephone Station. Since my communication soldiers used to work in the telephone station as operators, I was acquainted with the Eurasian and had even been invited to his home. I played cards with his two daughters, one with red hair, the other with black. The girls were very cheerful, joining in playing card tricks. Since the Allied Forces had advanced to Medan British soldiers had begun visiting the Eurasian's home. The

Indonesian youths who disliked this, attacked the house when the British soldiers were there. The soldiers escaped and the Indonesians captured three Tommy guns they left behind. The Indonesians tied the Eurasian girls' hands behind their backs and bound them to a tree in the garden.

When I thought of those innocent girls bound to a tree, crying helplessly as they watched their home burning, I felt an unbearable compassion and said, "Why do you treat such innocent girls so badly? They are to be pitied, aren't they?"

In response, the youths answered, "They deserved the punishment because they were intimate with the enemy."

Eurasian people were half Dutch and half Indonesian. Because Dutch policy gave them Dutch citizenship, they were proud of their superior position during Dutch rule. When the Japanese army landed, they cooperated with us, stressing that they were half Asian. When we lost the war and the Allied Forces advanced to Sumatra, they could not help welcoming the British. What would be their fate in the future? They were thus attacked by the Indonesians. Even if they were to go to the Netherlands, claiming that they were Dutch, there would be no guarantees that as half Asians they could enjoy life on a comparable level to the Dutch. I deeply sympathized with the Eurasians.

ANNA Is KIDNAPPED

Another curious thing began happening. It was kidnapping, and it caused panic among the Chinese and Eurasians. While they wanted to be protected by the Allied Forces, the RAPWI Camp was too small to admit all of them, and the Allied Forces did not intend to take responsibility for those living outside the camp.

One day a Eurasian girl named Anna was kidnapped from a house where she was visiting a friend and was lost for nearly ten days. Her father was a sergeant in the Dutch army, captured by the Japanese army and sent to construct the Thai-Burma railroad. Her mother kept house, and the two daughters worked for the Japanese military government as typists. Because their home was close to our barracks when I was living in Medan, I was acquainted with the family. Anna had a darker skin than most Eurasians and was an innocent and obedient girl of around 16 years. Because she was not that pretty, most boys did not like to dance with her and she spent most of her time operating the record player. Nevertheless, she was extremely fond of dance parties. Her personality was very optimistic and good-hearted and she never missed the birthday parties of her friends. I could not understand why such a nice girl was a target of the Indonesian youths. So I complained to the youths of the intelligence unit, "Why did you kidnap such an innocent girl who thinks nothing of political affairs? There is no possibility that such a girl would work for NICA as a spy or whatever."

The youths answered with a sarcastic smile, "We do not know because we were not the kidnappers. Why are you so concerned about a Eurasian girl who is Dutch?"

Anna, however, was released and returned home a short time later, though I do not know if it was the result of my complaint or not. Because I was informed of her release by the youths, I dropped by her home. Her house was one of the high-floored wooden homes lining the left side of the road to Delitua. The room over the front steps was a lobby and inside was a dining room with bedrooms on both sides.

Although nearly a year had passed since I visited the house before the end of the war, no change was evident. The whole family warmly welcomed me -- an officer of the defeated enemy -- with no change in their attitude. I was taken into the dining room to avoid the visibility of the outside lobby. I first expressed my sympathies to the kidnapped Anna. She sadly smiled to thank me but did not intend to talk about anything that happened with the kidnapping. From her sorrowful appearance, I could guess how dreadfully this innocent girl had been treated during her kidnapping and felt an unbearable grief for her.

THE TRAGEDY OF ANNA'S FATHER

Anna had an older sister named Elly. Elly was much fairer than Anna but she was also not very pretty and never failed to go to church every Sunday. She was an excellent pianist but moderate in all things and did not like to dance. She had a clear head and had mastered the Japanese language very quickly by studying enthusiastically after she was affiliated with the Japanese military government. Elly was carefully observing the faces of Anna and me from a seat at the side. When her mother left the room to prepare some tea, she suddenly said to me in Japanese, while sensitive to my position, "Capt. Fusayama, our father has come back from Burma."

Oh yes, I remembered that their father, who was a Eurasian with Dutch nationality, had been called by the Dutch army to fight against the Japanese, had been imprisoned by the Japanese, and sent to Burma to construct a railroad over the mountains. Their father was released after the Japanese surrendered and returned home. I expressed my hearty congratulations on his safe return, "Is that so? Safely? Congratulations."

Although I said this heartily, my body felt a chill and I did not know what to do next. The Thai-Burma railroad was planned by the Japanese army after facing difficulty in obtaining supplies due to the marine blockade. It was extremely hard work and a project beyond common sense. The rails were supplied from those taken out of railroad branches in Malaya and Java. All other materials were local products. The road was constructed along mountain ridges. Bombing by Allied Forces' airplanes made the work even more difficult. Even within the Japanese army, many soldiers died from malaria and malnutrition because of a lack of food supplies. Since even the Japanese soldiers suffered in this way, the suffering experienced by the prisoners who worked under the Japanese soldiers was beyond our estimation. Anna's sister, Elly, politely thanked me for my congratulations, but soon after said to me, "My father does not want to see you. He is lying on the bed in the next room."

I lost my presence of mind in shock, feeling as though cold water had been poured over me. It was quite natural. His grudge towards the Japanese was reasonable. In constructing the Thai-Burma railroad through the tropical mountain forests, how hard had it been for the father of these daughters? The peaceful, happy home life of this family was completely destroyed by the Japanese invasion of Sumatra. How miserable was the tormented life of a prisoner? How sad was the separation of husband and wife, parent and daughters for four years. He could finally return home, but his beloved teenage daughter was kidnapped by the Indonesians. There was no way of rescuing his daughter, however much he wanted. How long would this hard time last? The Japanese were responsible for all of these disasters. A member of the Japanese army, who could never be cursed enough, was now sitting in his own home with a shameless smile.

How was the father feeling now, listening to my voice? In the silent next room, he might be desperately bearing his grief by covering himself with a blanket. Or, he might be glaring at a corner of the ceiling with his teeth fiercely clenched. I stood up in consternation, feeling that I was in a place to which I should not have come.

BEYOND THE HATRED

When I was about to excuse myself, Elly asked me to wait after a whisper from her mother, "Just a moment please."

Elly and her mother brought a handful of tobacco. Surprised, I said, "Oh no, please use it for yourself because I am not a smoker." But Elly said gently and resolutely, "I know you do not smoke. But, please, give it to your pitiful soldiers who were defeated in this war. They must be short of tobacco."

They kept bringing tobacco, forming a mound on the table. With a cord to tie it in her hands, the mother, smiling like the Holy Mother, watched her daughters wrap the tobacco in papers. Although the tobacco was a humble native product seized by the Dutch army from the Japanese storage house, tears almost flooded my eyes.

What pure love was this! There was no enemy and friend. Neither nations nor races. The noble, pure, and clean love from human to human was shining warmly. I recalled that this family were sincere Christians. The beautiful heart. The noble love. However, the love was not a creation of Christ. The warm blood of love has been pulsing in the human vessels for eternity. The misfortunes of humans happen when love is overcome by hatred. The father seemed to be desperately coping by giving over his hatred to his daughters' love.

Returning to the liaison office, I myself, who had been pitied by Anna's family, deeply pitied them in return, thinking of the family's future. This family of mixed blood had been happy in their superior position during the period of Dutch rule. With Indonesia opening the fire of the independence war against the Dutch, however, I wondered if they would continue to be happy, either by going to the Netherlands or staying in Sumatra. Although they were Dutch citizens, that fifty percent of their blood was Indonesian was an absolute fact. How does Anna's father regard the independence movement? The happiness of Eurasian families such as Anna's cannot be expected until the day comes when the Dutch and Indonesians can grip each other's hands.

CHAPTER THIRTEEN
THE DISTRESS OF A FREEDOM FIGHTER

THE LOVE OF A GUERRILLA FIGHTER

Among the young men of the Fifth Corps intelligence unit who should have been fighting cheerfully, there was one youth suffering from unexpected distress. This was Jusuf, a light-skinned, sociable young man who used to work at the Estate Control Bureau before the war ended. When the war was over, he was discharged and returned to Sibolga, a port town on the Indian Ocean, to stay with his father who owned a rubber estate. When Jusuf heard that the independence war had started in Medan, he returned there with a burning passion and joined the Fifth Corps alongside his old friends. His elderly father was, however, anxious that his important only son withdraw from the Fifth Corps and return home, and every time he came to Medan, he pleaded unsuccessfully with his son to do so.

Even among the Batak, there were quite a few unusually fair-skinned people from the district of Batak Angkola. Jusuf had a fair-skinned, slim, and delicate body and a sociable and indecisive personality, characteristic of the indulged son of a wealthy family. Living away from his parents, he always wore a dirty white shirt. He listened silently to his father's pleas without replying, but he never said that he would return home.

I became acquainted with him after the war's end. He respected me very much, as did his friends, and always received me with warmth and politeness. Opening his heart to me, he sometimes talked of the interesting customs of the Angkola Batak in his native district. The Batak people, who kept their traditional culture isolated from the outside for nearly a thousand years, had a surprisingly romantic custom. Their society was governed by traditional customary law (*adat*), that regulated even love affairs precisely. In the love talk between boy and girl, regular conversation was never used but feelings were exchanged in singing improvised poems just like in the Mannyo Age, 1,300 years ago in Japan. In the Batak villages of huge houses and steep rafters surrounded by thick, dark woods, a man and a woman would slowly approach each other under the mysterious moonlight, dancing softly and singing their spontaneous made-up songs. It was like a scene from a dream world. Jusuf's fantastic and mysterious stories pleased me because of my study of Batak folklore. When he was telling me the story, his heart seemed to open up completely to me. Nevertheless, when I mentioned his father's wishes, he closed his mouth determinedly and switched the topic of conversation.

After some days, I found out that he had a reason, other than the independence movement, not to leave Medan. He had a girlfriend in the town. It was a modern, free type of love, far different from the dreamy, traditional love in his native Batak village. His lover was a Eurasian girl named Merry. It was certainly a problem for a member of the youth party fighting for independence to love a girl of Dutch nationality.

A Freedom Fighter and his Lover Living in the RAPWI Camp

Her skin was a shiny, copper-brown and her long, slim limbs always looked alive and fresh. Her lively figure with long legs under her gay colored skirt gave her the image of a dancing angel from a southern country. So she was nicknamed Josephine Baker, the name of an American entertainer who was world famous at that time. Because I sometimes used to visit the Estate Control Bureau in Medan where she was working, I had seen her casually. Jusuf, who happened to work as a clerk in the room next to hers, got to know her, and finally fell in love. When the war was over they were already engaged. Unfortunately, however, she lived with her family in the RAPWI camp, protected by the Dutch army as a Dutch citizen.

INDEPENDENCE AND LOVE

When I heard of this relationship, I was very anxious about Jusuf's delicate situation. But Jusuf's analysis of his position was surprisingly clear. He emphatically explained his patriotic resolution to join the independence movement regardless of his personal relationship with the Dutch girl, clearly distinguishing between his public and private affairs. At the same time, however, he never thought of abandoning his fiancée. While participating in guerrilla attacks as a freedom fighter, he was also racking his brains to find a way of meeting Merry who was staying in the RAPWI camp.

He stated his opinion to me in an unusually decisive manner, placing his fist on the table: "I am Indonesian. When Indonesia proclaimed independence, I joined the movement, overcoming all my personal feelings. My passion for independence is never subordinated to other people. I am devoting myself to independence together with my comrades. However, as a human being, in my private life I must be permitted to love any girl. Our love across national boundaries will not change anything. Public and private are separated. I can clearly distinguish between public and private affairs. What do you think? I think you will agree with me."

He thus hoped that I would agree. I felt as if I was hearing a speech from a romance in a cheap girls' magazine. Since we Japanese were still somewhat inhibited in our personal lives, and had not completely freed ourselves from the social concepts of a feudalistic age, I thought it was necessary for us to learn something from more idealistic concepts. However, Jusuf's ideas were unrealistic. Although it is desirable to distinguish between public and private life, no one's private life can be completely free from his public life. At the same time, it is impossible for a human being to carry on a public life while completely neglecting a private life. In particular, a person of weak character cannot help being governed by the real world regardless of the ideals he dreams of. I was not moved by Jusuf's words because I knew his character was weak. His words sounded lovely, but he was a weak man. Although I believed he really meant what he said at the moment, I wondered how long he would be able to bear the dilemma. I could not be confident in him but I could not hate him either. Anyway, I answered him with a wry smile, "Yes, you are right."

I simply could not find any other answer. Delighted with my response, Jusuf talked about various other aspects of his love affair, even things I did not ask about.

JUSUF'S LOVER APPEARS

One day when I was talking with the youths of the intelligence unit, Merry's face suddenly appeared in the window. She was short of breath because she had come here secretly to see her lover, stealing out of the RAPWI camp evading the guard of the Dutch soldiers. Jusuf's comrades kidded him as he shouted for joy. He called without reserve, "Hey, Merry!"

He jumped up and hastily drew her into the room through the back door. Merry told him -- in what seemed to be the Dutch language -- of her painful effort to get there, while busily touching the collar and other parts of Jusuf's clothing in a manner of uncontrollable delight.

Jusuf's comrades left the room one after another. I was stupid enough not to recognize until too late that I should also leave so as not to disturb the couple. When I stood up, however, Jusuf said to me hastily, "We don't mind if you stay. Nothing will be secret from you. Please feel free to be seated."

He meant that I was specially permitted to remain there. I was honored and curious. Although I knew it was not smart, I decided to stay and observe their love affair. I was still a bachelor. If I were back in Japan and released from the army, a sweet love would be waiting for me. So, I sat down again. However, since the very open affection between the couple affected me too much, I could not move at all, sinking deep into the sofa.

When there was a pause in their conversation, she saw for the first time that I was sitting on the sofa. She acknowledged me with a smile. Jusuf introduced me to her since this was the first time that I had actually met her. Because I was being spoken to by such a charming girl who looked like an angel from heaven, I was embarrassed and answered in a mix of English, German, and Indonesian. She was pleased and startled when I inserted a few Dutch words in various places. Damn! What a fresh and cheerful girl she was! My heart became hot. I began to feel jealous of Jusuf who sat beside the angel with a confident smile.

DON'T ABANDON THE FATHERLAND

Thereafter, on the pretext of having something to talk about with her former supervisor from the Estate Control Bureau who happened to work in our liaison office, Merry was able occasionally to come and see Jusuf.

Some time later, Jusuf came to consult with me with a very troubled look, "Merry's family is repatriating to the Netherlands. Her parents are going to take Merry with them no matter what. What shall I do?"

It was a very difficult question. Nevertheless, I gave him a very decisive answer, being somewhat influenced by my jealousy.

"If Merry is willing to be completely devoted to you, she should come to you and abandon her family. If she wants to go to the Netherlands with her family, it is proof that her love for you is not stable. You should abandon such a girl in that case. You are a man. Don't pursue a girl who is leaving. I do not believe you are a man who would abandon his fatherland to run after a woman."

"You are right, of course," he answered. But, as he left, he looked extremely sad.

In the meantime, the Dutch had become nervous that the Eurasians and Ambonese who had been connected with the Japanese during the occupation still liked to come to our liaison office and continue their friendships with the Japanese. They severely restricted their movements, and, as a result, Merry could no longer come to see Jusuf. Unbearably lonely, Jusuf began to visit Merry secretly in the RAPWI camp. I thought it was very dangerous. If the Dutch intelligence unit noticed and wanted to use him, what would happen? I felt very anxious, afraid of such results.

My anxiety was noticed by Jusuf, too. He was most afraid that I, his respected friend, would doubt his patriotism. Consequently, he expressed his hope that I would believe his theory of distinguishing between the public and the private. The more he repeated his position, however, the more uncertain I felt. I therefore hesitated to please him simply by saying, "Yes, sure, I believe you."

However, one day I said to him teasing, "*Ya, saya percaya* [Yes, I believe you]." After seeing his delighted face, I went on, "*Percaya Jusuf orang nakal* [I believe Jusuf is a naughty boy]."

He replied with sour smile, "Oh, don't joke. Don't tease me. But, your joking with me is proof that we are close and that you believe me."

Thus agreeing with himself, he scratched his head.

CHAPTER FOURTEEN
THE JAPANESE WITHDRAWAL FROM ACEH

THE JAPANESE ARMY IS WITHDRAWN

While I was busily settling the Tebing incident, the withdrawal of the Japanese army from Aceh, which the Allied Forces had permitted as a result of my desperate efforts, was being prepared. Governor Hasan came back from his tour through Aceh to persuade the Acehnese to secure the safe withdrawal of the Japanese.

However, the bloody struggle in Aceh between the Ulebalang and PUSA was continuing, and Japanese arms were desperately being sought. Therefore, it would be very difficult to prevent trouble if the Japanese army were to withdraw the long way by land. At the very least, it was certain that a great number of weapons would get into the hands of the Acehnese. The Allied Forces, who were most afraid of that happening, therefore ordered the Japanese to withdraw by sea from their individual posts.

On December 18, the day after peace was restored to Tebing Tinggi, one battalion of the 4th Imperial Guard Infantry Regiment staying in the area of Kota Raja, first embarked on a ship under the cover of a British destroyer and went to Malaya. On December 23, one company of the Japanese Marine Transportation Troops left Sigli by sea and landed in Pangkalan Brandan to join up with the main force of their 4th Infantry Regiment. One battalion of the 3rd Imperial Guard Infantry Regiment, stationed in Lhokseumawe and Bireuen, had gathered in Lhokseumawe, waiting for the boats of the Marine Transportation Troop to come for them on the night of December 24. Only one battalion of the 3rd Regiment stationed in Langsa, close to East Sumatra Province, withdrew by train.

We were particularly anxious about the safety of the troops withdrawing from Lhokseumawe because they had been completely disarmed. The withdrawal order was sent by wireless and the boats planned to approach the coast of Lhokseumawe secretly. With intense anxiety, the divisional headquarters waited for a report of the safe departure of the troops. I, myself, however, was not at all anxious because I trusted the report from Governor Hasan that he had reached an agreement with the Acehnese in various places to secure the lives and property of the withdrawing Japanese.

Nevertheless, at midnight I was told of an express order from the divisional headquarters by Staff Officer Imamura, who was also the director of our liaison office: "We have had wireless confirmation that the troops from Lhokseumawe have safely boarded boats. But wireless communication has been lost. We cannot confirm their departure. Since the telephone network is under the control of the Acehnese, please ask your Indonesian friends to confirm by telephone whether the Japanese troops have safely departed from Lhokseumawe."

I was reluctant to do so and replied, "I do not think we should ask the Indonesians for such a confirmation, because the boats will arrive in the Pangkalan Brandan port tomorrow morning. We can confirm it for ourselves then."

Seeing my hesitation, Staff Officer Imamura finally said: "Although I did not tell you earlier because it was very secret, the 5th Regiment is ready to launch a sudden attack on Langsa. The regiment passed secretly through Delitua and Arnemia, avoiding Medan, and is now waiting in Kuala Simpang adjacent to the provincial border with Aceh. If they advance before the troops in Lhokseumawe have departed, those troops will be in serious danger. Please check it out quickly."

I was very surprised and refused. "What? What a terribly dishonest thing this is! When the Acehnese are allowing all Japanese troops to leave safely under the direction of Governor Hasan, who trusted me, you are immediately responding with an attack! I can never cooperate in such a betrayal."

I refused, turning very red. Staff Officer Imamura, however, pleaded with me: "I understand. I know you are right. But, please consider this. When we were permitted to withdraw our troops from Aceh, we were in serious trouble with the Allied Forces over the great amount of arms that were handed over to the Acehnese in violation of the surrender agreement. If we do not do anything about that, our division has no more excuses. In addition, more arms were taken from the troops leaving Langsa. We cannot report to the Allied Forces without having taken some counteraction. The 5th Regiment has finished deployment and is ready to start. The divisional order can no longer be withdrawn. If we do not hurry to confirm the departure of the Lhokseumawe troops, there may be serious confusion. The regiment is ready to depart. Please, please help us."

I suffered unbearably from the bitterness of betraying Governor Hasan whom I considered a very close friend. I recalled the bitterness of "Lawrence of Arabia" that I had once read about. The 5th Regiment by now was almost ready to advance. The troops in Lhokseumawe were on the verge of being in serious danger. With heartbreaking grief, I made up my mind to betray my friend in order to save the soldiers in Lhokseumawe. Desperately repressing my exploding self-reproach, I telephoned the Indonesian operator at the Medan Telephone Station and asked for a check on Lhokseumawe. I did not ask my friends in the intelligence unit because I did not want to drive my dear friends into a corner when the matter became known by the public.

The operator kindly called Lhokseumawe to check, without raising any suspicions. The troops had already left by boat and not a single soldier remained in the barracks.

ADVANCE TO LANGSA

The 5th Imperial Guard Infantry Regiment commanded by Maj. Gen. Sawamura immediately advanced to Langsa. It was December 25. Langsa was deserted except for a few scouts who were easily driven away. Although no arms were retrieved, the regiment did not push further. After staying in Langsa for only one day, it quickly returned to Kuala Simpang. Only a few Japanese were wounded or killed, and the Indonesian casualties seemed also to be not very many.

I felt relieved to know that no serious battle took place between the Japanese and Acehnese. Meanwhile, I received a phone call from Kuala Simpang. It was a request from Maj. Gen. Sawamura, "I would like to organize a remedial negotiation with Aceh. Please come to Kuala Simpang accompanied by Governor Hasan."

I immediately conveyed this request to the governor and the next day we arrived in Kuala Simpang in two cars. Maj. Gen. Sawamura had established the regiment's headquarters in a big one-story house located in the center of town. We were shown into a wide lobby-like drawing room with a high ceiling. The regiment commander, Sawamura, soon came in, accompanied by his adjutant, and sat in front of Hasan. I sat by Hasan to interpret. Several officers and others from the headquarters stood around us tensely. A huge tropical fan was quietly revolving in the center of the ceiling.

I was afraid that Governor Hasan would not be comfortable alone among so many Japanese soldiers. But, as soon as the meeting opened, he boldly protested the betrayal by the Japanese army.

"Trusting the promise that I made with the Japanese army through Capt. Fusayama, I took the trouble to go to Aceh to persuade the Acehnese people to secure the safe withdrawal of the Japanese army. Nevertheless, you attacked Langsa immediately after all the troops were safely withdrawn. This is a very unjust betrayal."

As I translated his charge, I felt ashamed of the Japanese army and of myself. Surprisingly, however, Maj. Gen. Sawamura refuted him quite composedly and without flinching: "No, it isn't. The betrayers were the Acehnese. You promised to secure the lives and property of the withdrawing troops. However, the Acehnese in Langsa stole not only arms, but also the personal property of the Japanese soldiers despite the agreement. How could we overlook such a betrayal?"

I was very surprised by the logic of his rebuttal and his cleverness. Actually, the soldiers withdrawing from Langsa had been robbed not only of binoculars and water bottles, but also watches and purses. Some soldiers were half-naked, having had even their shirts seized. I heartily but silently appreciated that the Acehnese dared pillage in this way.

RECLAIMING THE ARMS

Maj. Gen. Sawamura further charged: "Under the surrender agreement, we promised the Allied Forces to keep all our arms to surrender to them. We are obliged to take back our arms from the Acehnese. I did not chase the Acehnese beyond Langsa to take back arms because I did not want to kill Acehnese. Instead of fighting further, I ask you to persuade the

Acehnese to give the arms back. Otherwise, we cannot help but advance not only to Langsa, but further on deep into Aceh."

Governor Hasan gave no answer, his mouth tightly closed. I thought to myself that this would never be possible. The Acehnese, who are fighting for independence with their lives, will never return the arms that they obtained through so much effort. This was an unreasonable demand. Such a demand was unthinkable for someone who heartily hoped for the success of Indonesian independence. I was cornered by the dilemma between my own wishes and the words I was interpreting.

Suddenly, however, as a last resort I had an idea, thinking about the personality of Maj. Gen. Sawamura. I entreated Governor Hasan with my mouth close to his ear, "It might only have to be a small amount. It will be enough if you bring back a few arms."

Hasan looked at me for a while and then stared at Sawamura. He finally stood up and left Kuala Simpang in his car, driving across the bridge of the provincial border guarded by Japanese soldiers.

We waited for him, holding our breath. Not long after noon on the next day, the car came back bearing a bitter-faced Governor Hasan.

Hasan did not say anything to us when we came out to see him. His driver went to the back of the car and opened the trunk. The armory officer took out the contents, assisted by his soldiers. They found twenty Japanese infantry rifles, Type 38, but all were broken and useless.

The officer became angry and went to the regiment commander's room, reporting, "Your Excellency, there are only twenty returned rifles. All of them are broken."

The officers in the room watched the face of their commander expecting an angry response. The commander, Sawamura, however, did not get angry. Instead, he stood up with a grin and soothed his staff, saying, "Its all right."

He then went to Governor Hasan who had just come into the drawing room and shook his hand to thank him, "Your effort is appreciated."

I knew that this result was just what he expected. The 5th Regiment had indeed taken back some arms. This would prove that they made an effort. The regiment could send a reasonable report now to the division headquarters as well as to the Allied Forces. Relieved of tension, I returned to Medan together with Governor Hasan. The Acehnese people did not thereafter cause any trouble with the Japanese.

THE UNITED ACEHNESE

On returning to Medan, I recommended to the division through Staff Officer Imamura, that my old friend Muramoto, the civil administrator who had just retired from Aceh, be appointed the director of a special agency to keep in contact with Aceh in Kuala Simpang. In our Acehnese military government, he had shown a special ability in training the Acehnese youth for administration and also in manipulating the local governing class, the Ulebalang. As I expected, former Japanese secret agents, such as Sergeant Shima, who had been secretly cooperating with the Acehnese independence movement, came to cooperate with Muramoto in the office, disguising themselves as Indonesians. And various Acehnese freedom fighters began to communicate with the Japanese through them. Although our army had been ordered by the Allied Forces to arrest such Japanese deserters, we all pretended not to notice them.

Once the troops had been withdrawn from Aceh, the serious struggle between the Ulebalang and PUSA that was particularly serious in north-central Aceh, was drawing to a close. In the district of Bireuen, PUSA destroyed the Ulebalang forces in a sudden attack on their base. In the district of Sigli too, the Ulebalang forces were finally destroyed. The Sigli district controller, Teuku Cu Hasan, who was the supreme leader, was killed, together with all the other adults of the Ulebalang group. Even Hasan's ten-year-old son reportedly had his testicles removed. It was literally an extirpation.

In other districts, however, the struggle between Ulebalang and PUSA was not as serious, and the people reached an overall agreement under the direction of intelligent youths from the Ulebalang families who were officers in the TKR, once trained by the Japanese army. Aceh thus reached a general unity and became the most stable base for the independence struggle. Consequently, a great number of Japanese deserters successively came to Aceh and engaged in various functions such as repairing weapons, producing explosives, military training, etc. Aceh earnestly prepared for a future decisive battle against the Dutch. The defense that was established was strong enough to prevent the Dutch forces from putting foot in the province until the end -- even when all the other areas of Indonesia had been occupied by the Dutch Second Action in 1948.

CHAPTER FIFTEEN
THE DECLINE OF THE FIFTH CORPS

THE ASSASSINATION OF SIHITE

On the morning of the last day of 1945, the day after I returned from Kuala Simpang, I woke up unusually late and paid a visit to the intelligence unit to catch up on what had happened in the time I was away.

When I went in, something completely unexpected had happened. Boyke Nainggolan the second son of Dr. Nainggolan, was talking on the telephone and almost in tears. All the other members of the group were slouched on the sofas, holding their heads in their hands. I asked them, "What is the matter, what has happened?"

One of them responded to my question, almost sobbing, "The situation is awful. Our commander, Sihite, is lost. Our vice-commander, Dr. Nainggolan, has been arrested."

Bob Nainggolan, the first son of Dr. Nainggolan, was sitting on a sofa with bloodshot eyes, not saying anything and holding his head in both hands. His brother, Boyke, talking on the telephone, was dressed in an overcoat despite the tropical heat because he had a fever raging at 39° C. His eyes were bloodshot and his voice was rasping:

"Hello, Mama. Hello! Mama! What happened after that? Eh? I can't hear. Hello, Mama. Can you hear me? Hello? Hello, Mama? Who took my father away? Eh? What? Did you say unknown? Why unknown? Why, Mama? Helpless. Um....Ah, Mama? This is Boyke speaking. This is Boyke. Boyke Nainggolan. What? Who are you? Hello. Hello. There is nothing. Hello, Mama? There is nothing, the line has been cut. Someone has cut it. Ah, I feel so helpless."

Hanging the receiver back on the hook, Boyke fell into a nearby chair and coughed painfully, almost as if his breathing had stopped.

The youths narrated the following story to me. Last night, their commander, Sihite, and vice-commander, Dr. Nainggolan, went up to Brastagi in the cool Karo Highlands, to take a few days rest for the New Year, away from the riots and attacks in Medan. Brastagi was a cool, highland resort 60 kilometers from Medan, 1,200 meters above sea level and surrounded by high mountains such as Mt. Sinabung -- nicknamed Sumatra Fuji by the Japanese -- and Mt. Sibayak, a volcano called the Mountain of the King. Because the highlands were cool like the autumn in Japan, most of the Dutch had villas there to enjoy on the weekends. Sihite lodged in a Chinese hotel called Hotel Mata Hari, and Dr. Nainggolan went to his own villa where his wife and daughter were living.

At midnight, a group of armed Indonesians suddenly rushed into the Nainggolans' residence, breaking down the front door and taking away Dr. Nainggolan who was in bed with his wife. Bob and Boyke's mother was terrified at first. She then recovered her senses and called her sons in Medan on the telephone. But the telephone was not functioning during the night. So the mother waited until morning without sleeping. When the telephone was working again in the morning, Bob and Boyke found out what had happened. The youths cried out, "This is awful! This is terrible! Our commander Sihite is facing great danger."

The youths of the Fifth Corps became very nervous and telephoned Sihite's hotel, but Sihite had already disappeared without a trace. Nainggolan's sons repeatedly telephoned their mother, but no definite information was obtained. Meanwhile, the operator disconnected the line to their mother. The situation was very serious. I sat down on a sofa and asked, "What do you think has happened?" The youths replied, "We do not know at all what the matter is. However, we believe that a man like Sihite can never be easily captured or killed. Because he is very shrewd, we are sure he must have escaped and is now hiding somewhere. Because Nainggolan was captured, he must be a prisoner somewhere. The attackers were probably Pesindo or the TKR. Mrs. Nainggolan said she thought a Japanese deserter was leading the group."

Bob Nainggolan, the elder brother, said that he wanted to go to Brastagi to look for his father. Boyke, who was suffering from a high fever, staggered up and croaked, "Brother, I also want to go to save Papa."

Two of the other youths also decided to go with the brothers. In my deep sympathy for them, I gave them liberal amounts of fuel for their car and a certificate so they would not be stopped by Japanese sentries on the way.

When I saw Governor Hasan for our periodic meeting later that afternoon, I asked him, "Whatever happened to Sihite?" Surprised for a moment, he spat out a reply, "Oh, you know about that already? He was a secret agent of NICA. I would not care if he was dead."

As I felt that something secret was going on, I left without further touching on the subject.

THE FIFTH CORPS LOSE THEIR COMMANDER

After several days, the youths who went to look for Sihite and Nainggolan returned to Medan and said, "As we expected, Sihite has not been captured. Because he is very shrewd, he must be hiding somewhere."

Although they said this, a rumor that Sihite was dead began to spread in the streets. After some time, even the youths of the Fifth Corps ceased to deny that Sihite had died

One day, a Medan newspaper, *Suara Merdeka* (Voice of Independence), published the following announcement:

> Pasukan Kelima (the Fifth Corps of the Youth Party) have lost their commander. Because of all the bad rumors, we are taking this opportunity to disband the Fifth Corps. We will make a new start with *Singa Nasional*, and we will further strengthen the independence movement. Our new commander is Huta Julu.

I knew that Singa meant lion. It must have been taken from *Singa Mangaraja* (the Great Lion King), who was a leader of the traditional religion that the Batak people followed, and was also a national hero who had resisted Dutch aggression until the last fight in 1907. On reading this news I went over to the intelligence unit. The youths there had sour faces. "This news is true. We think you know the meaning of Singa because you have studied Batak folklore. The name is great. However, we prefer our original name, Pasukan Kelima. You wait and see." They did not talk about it anymore.

When I visited them two days later, they were celebrating.

"You see? We have restored Pasukan Kelima. Remember we said to wait and see? Boyke is a very brave man. Boyke did it. We all helped. Huta Julu, who became the head of Singa Nasional, is extremely bad. When Sihite got into trouble in Brastagi, he did not attempt to save him, but rather took over the leadership position instead. It should have been the first vice-commander, Dr. Nainggolan, who took over when Sihite died. If he could not, then the second vice-commander, Nirwan, should take the position. However, Huta Julu, head of the police section, took it over after conspiring with two other men. Dr. Nainggolan's son, Boyke, became very angry and secretly planned an attack with our help. The conspirators are now being held in Medan Prison.

We also have some other big news. Dr. Nainggolan, who had been confined in Brastagi, has been released. Three of our comrades went to receive him. Pasukan Kelima will continue under the leadership of Dr. Nainggolan."

Although Boyke was in Brastagi greeting his father, I recalled the figure sick with fever on the telephone the other day. In admiration I imagined him rushing into the three-day-old rebellion headquarters, pointing his pistol at the chest of the rebels, shouting, "Hold up your hands!"

However, I did wonder if they really knew the minds of their former commander, Sihite, and their father, Nainggolan. I sadly questioned whether Sihite and Nainggolan were freedom fighters as they believed. I prayed that Nainggolan, at least, was a real freedom fighter and that he would not betray the trust of his fine sons. I could not help being caught up by a feeling of suspicion, however much I tried to dismiss it. I was afraid that a judgment day would come when everything would be revealed to them.

THE JAVANESE YOUTH, SIDIK

Since Sihite, who had commanded both Pesindo and Pasukan Kelima, was dead, Sarwono became the commander of Pesindo which, from then on, disassociated itself from the Fifth Corps. Consequently, I wished to make contact with the reorganized youth party as a way of preventing trouble between the Indonesian youths and the Japanese army. Because the location of the party's headquarters was kept secret, I visited the police section of the party, located in the center of the town.

The young man who met me at the front desk was a Javanese named

Sidik, whom I had once trained as a Heiho. When he saw my face, he cried in Japanese, "*Kyokan Dono* [my teacher]!" And he gratefully received me with a salute to his cap.

Of Sidik, I have the following memory: Before the war was over, I had trained the Heiho as an officer attached to the headquarters of the Imperial Guard Division's communications troops. One day I went on a round of the Heiho barracks, while my assistant was training them in the field. The barracks were a house with a roof of nipa palm tree leaves, built on a lawn overlooking a curve in the Babura River, east of the official guest house in Medan. At the side of the river 30 meters away, there was a toilet house and a wash place with a water faucet. I happened to notice a small Heiho figure looking up at me, crouching on the wet concrete floor.

"What is the matter with you?" I asked him as I approached. His expressionless face moved slightly and he silently pointed to his shin. An awful tropical ulcer had spread over the entire surface of both shins. Pus was flowing from various parts of the ulcerated surface and his muscles had become hollow from decomposition, the bone almost exposed. Tropical ulcers were a very dirty, chronic disease that was caused by a kind of spirochate and was very difficult to cure because of a lack of effective medicine. Our medical orderlies treated the ulcers by washing them with clean water and coating them daily with drugs that were available, but it often took a few months to cure. Though not painful, as is usual with diseases of spirochates, the patient's physical strength was considerably depleted when the disease lasted a long time. Sidik had been ordered to rest from drill and had been lying by himself in the barracks. When he came to the toilet and washed his hands, he lacked the strength to walk back.

I felt a surge of pity for this small-bodied Javanese youth who looked more like a child and thought to myself: He has a home in his village; it may be a small cottage, but his mother would be there. Responding to the propaganda of the Japanese military government to defend his country, without thinking too much he had volunteered for the Heiho. Although he looked cheerful when training and in good health, he was now seriously sick. How lonely, sad, and helpless must he feel when left alone, sick, in the empty barracks? How anxious would his mother be if she knew this? All youths are somebody's child. I thought how we could not even guess the anxiety of his parents. I said to him, "Come, I will take you to bed."

I lifted up his body and carried him back to his bed in the barracks. His thin and weak body was frighteningly light. Since Sumatra was very warm, he wore nothing more than the knee-length trousers of thin blue cloth that were the Heiho uniform. He hardly moved when I held him. His naked skin on the upper half of his body was cool and wet. He was completely silent. When I laid his body on his bed covered with a mat, he looked up at me expressionless, as if he did not understand what was happening.

However, the Sidik standing in front of me now looked cheerful and lively, as if he were a completely different man. He was now a freedom fighter for his fatherland, and, in high spirits, looked after the front desk of the police section of Pesindo. Gratefully, he passed on my wish and took me into his commander's room. Had he grown into an adult after only one year? Or does a man change this much because he is activated by his own passion? Anyway, the self-confidence with which Sidik welcomed me seemed like that of another person.

The commander of the police section of the youth party was also, unexpectedly, my acquaintance. He was a cousin, on his mother's side, of Nirwan, named Imbalo Effendi Harahap. His father was Maharaja Parlagutan Harahap. He was the person who told Nirwan the story of the Japanese deserters who had made the suicide attack on the British barracks.

I gripped his hand saying, "What a surprise, you are the commander." He was a diligent, serious youth. I had heard that he had passed the entrance examination for a college founded by the Japanese army in Singapore in only one try and had been studying there. He had returned to Medan before finishing college because the war ended. I found it interesting that Nirwan and Imbalo, who were cousins, were the leaders of Pasukan Kelima and Pesindo, which were now antagonistic to each other.

Another person who surprised me was his adjutant sitting at his side with a pistol at his waist. It was the stout, humorous man who used to be a comedian at a theater in Medan. The former comedian showed sufficient dignity to be one of the leaders of the police section of Pesindo. I was surprised at the great change in him, recalling how he had always moved the audience to laughter with his false tears on the stage. I had often visited the theater because I was fond of domestic comedies, so I had become acquainted with him too. I was thus immediately close to the people in the police section.

INTERVIEW WITH THE NEW COMMANDER OF PESINDO

Because I wanted to see the new commander of Pesindo, Sarwono, to establish ways to prevent unfortunate conflicts between Indonesian youths and the Japanese army, I asked Imbalo to arrange for an interview. Because Sarwono was being hunted by the Allied Forces, the emissaries of NICA, the Fifth Corps, etc., he hesitated to see me for a long time, fearing that he would be found by his enemies. Finally, on January 9, Imbalo came to me to say that the interview was ready. I asked him, "Where is the meeting place? Where is Sarwono now?" But Imbalo replied, "Please do not ask that. I was ordered to bring you without telling you the destination. Please come with me without asking questions."

There would be no way for me to be rescued in an emergency if I were to go without telling my comrades in the liaison office where I was going. It was still unknown whether Sarwono was pro- or anti-Japanese. It might be possible for him to capture me and force me to become a deserter and join his movement. I might be killed through some misunderstanding. In Medan at that time, more than a few people were being killed daily. Our lives were always exposed to danger.

However, I could understand also that Sarwono did not want his whereabouts known for the very same reason. I recalled a Japanese proverb saying, "*Koketsu ni irazunba koji o ezu* [A baby tiger cannot be caught without braving the danger of going into the tiger's lair]." Therefore, I had to go. Reconsidering the situation in this way, I wore civilian clothes with white trousers, instead of a regular military uniform, in order to look peaceful. But I did not forget to put a pistol secretly in my pocket. Asking the director of transportation in the liaison office to arrange for a car with the shrewdest driver, I followed Imbalo out of the office.

Imbalo led us endlessly left and right along the small roads to the east of Medan, but the place was easily identified because I was very familiar with Medan's geography. I had often enjoyed cycling through this area in the evening when I used to live in Medan.

When we arrived at one place, Sarwono had already moved on to another place, afraid that someone might be following our car. After another complicated drive, we arrived finally at the place for the interview. It was a residential area close to the south-eastern end of town, where some farms still remained in-between the houses. A single-story, Western-style building of white walls was located about 20 meters down from the road. Leaving us in our car, Imbalo went to the house to inform them of my arrival. While he was gone, I gave the following instructions to my driver, "If the situation becomes disorderly, I will shoot them and run out. Consequently, please wait for me with the door open and the engine running. If we go straight along this road, we can reach Ankara Street. Turning right, we then come to the Medan swimming pool. Keep this escape route in your mind." After giving those instructions to my driver, I went on down to the house.

I waited for a while, sitting on a wooden chair with a rattan seat, then the new commander of Pesindo, Sarwono, appeared, accompanied by several of his staff. The figure of Sarwono was much different from the boss-style I had guessed by analogy with Sihite. He was a slim, light-colored, handsome Javanese of around 34 or 35 years of age. He told me he used to be a teacher in Aceh. He looked like a clever, tactful man. It took me a moment to identify him as the commander from among the strong-looking officials guarding him. I extended my hand to him and smiled. He returned my handshake sociably and took his seat.

MY ADVICE TO INDONESIAN YOUTHS

After observing the personality of Sarwono, I began my business. After explaining the current position of the Japanese army -- having surrendered, yet being very sympathetic in our hearts towards the Indonesians -- I requested that he direct the youth party wisely so as not to cause a struggle between Indonesian and Japanese brothers. And, in order to prevent trouble arising from poor communication between the two, I proposed to him that he and I cooperate closely whenever any problems occurred. I further added the following advice: "Our Japanese army has been given the responsibility of maintaining public peace. We want peace also for the security of the Japanese people. The Pesindo youths, however, often cause trouble by randomly neglecting the policy of the

Indonesian government on various matters. This is not profitable, even for the independence struggle. Construction and production are more necessary than destruction. The independence war cannot be sustained for long without financial support. I cannot say that this advice will assist Indonesian independence because I am a member of the Japanese army that has been prohibited from assisting independence. I can only say that I wish it for the safe repatriation of Japanese. But you are the leaders of the Indonesian youth. Please be thoughtful. Please understand that we Japanese wish your movement success from the bottom of our hearts."

Sarwono listened to me, smiling. Then I lowered my voice and said, looking into his face, "I could not fully trust your predecessor, Sihite. I place a lot of hope in you, the new leader of this party."

A look that seemed to agree with my feelings appeared on his face. He was diametrically opposite to Sihite in his appearance, attitude, dress, and many other aspects. In contrast to Sihite, who had been taciturn with a dark air of suspicion, I felt that, under Sarwono, the new leadership would be forthright, pure, and reasonable. The staff, who had been standing around us in tension with their hands on their pistols, gradually relaxed their stance.

Sarwono leaned forward slightly and said to me, "Actually, I ordered the attack on him because he was an agent of NICA."

I replied, "I guessed that. The reason, perhaps, that you wanted to keep this meeting place so secret is that you are afraid of retaliation from the Fifth Corps?"

"Yes, you are right," answered Sarwono. "He was bought off by NICA and increased his power by secretly receiving funds and arms. He challenged the Japanese army as well as the Allied Forces in order to nip the independence movement in the bud by inviting the retaliation of the Japanese and British forces on the active Indonesians. Via a secret order from the government, I ordered Pesindo in Brastagi to arrest him. But they killed him by mistake. The youths who went to arrest him shot him dead. So, Sihite has died. I am taking the responsibility of revitalizing this party as its new commander."

The purpose of my interview was thus achieved perfectly. Fully relaxed, I gave him much advice for improving the independence movement, from a military, political, and financial perspective.

A STABILIZED YOUTH PARTY

Returning to the liaison office, I telephoned the garrison of Pangkalan Brandan which was the air defense regiment, and asked them to release the youths of the Pangkalan Brandan branch of Pesindo who had been imprisoned by the regiment after the riot at Tanjung Pura air base.

When the Japanese army fought with the Indonesian youths in Tebing Tinggi, the youths in Pangkalan Brandan attacked the Japanese air base defense troops in concert, and a Japanese officer, who happened to be out of the barracks for some fun that night, was killed. It was unknown by whom and how he was killed, but the regiment arrested the leaders of Pesindo as a warning, taking advantage of the strengthened position of the Japanese army after the Tebing incident. Sarwono had asked me to use my influence to get them released.

It was impossible for me to judge if they were responsible for the attack or not. However, even supposing that they were connected to it, they may have believed it necessary for independence and simply followed the standard beliefs at that time. The general situation had now completely changed, and the people knew that challenging the Japanese army could never be helpful to the independence movement. I thought, therefore, that it would be a good time to release them, even if they were responsible.

In response to my request, the regiment at Pangkalan Brandan immediately released them, because the regiment had been quite cooperative with me since my protest against the robbery of its soldiers. Imbalo then visited me to convey Sarwono's thanks. Cooperation between Sarwono and me thus began under very favorable conditions.

Thereafter, I used the home of Imbalo for communicating with Pesindo. Because repeated direct meetings were thought to be dangerous for both Sarwono and me, we agreed to maintain contact indirectly. That is, I met Imbalo at his home and he communicated with Sarwono. When Imbalo was absent, his sister, Sahara, kept me company until he returned. It was great fun for me to talk with the cheerful young girl. It made me recall my happy association with Indonesian girls and boys before the war ended.

These days I usually rode my bicycle around the city. I wore white civilian trousers to show my peacefulness to the Indonesian people and a green military uniform jacket to show the Allied Forces that I was moving around openly, without secrecy. But I surreptitiously carried a small pistol in the pocket of my trousers in case of emergency.

One day I took my leave, after enjoying a happy conversation with Sahara and her parents (Mr. and Mrs. Maharaja Parlagutan Harahap) at their house. When I was about to get on my bicycle, Sahara called me back with a teasing smile, "Sheiky [my nickname]. You left something behind."

Looking back, I found Sahara playfully pointing my pistol at me like a cowboy in a western movie. My pistol must have slipped out of my trousers when I was sitting down. Maharaja Parlagutan also joined in the joke, teasing me with a laugh, "If you do not need it, please donate it to us to use in the independence movement."

I left the house blushing. Imbalo, however, was always extremely earnest with me, in contrast to his sister and father. Without even a smile, he saw me off politely and sincerely.

A few days after our interview, Sarwono toured with his staff through various parts of East Sumatra Province to instruct the branches of Pesindo. As a result, the actions of the youth party stabilized considerably, and the trouble between the Japanese and Indonesians completely disappeared. Newspapers reported the instructions from the Pesindo leaders:

> The independence movement is not simply running around with bamboo spears. In order to achieve ultimate victory and continue this war of independence, we must save our national power by increasing production. All individuals must discharge their proper duties. Do not divide the Indonesian nation. Let us fight unified against one enemy. Do not destroy. Let us construct.

They were excellent instructions. I felt a rising love for the pureness and activeness of the young Indonesian leaders who were so obediently accepting and carrying out my advice, regardless of the fact that I was a mere amateur in politics. The childish guerrilla attacks that had prevailed in Medan had almost disappeared and bigger conflicts, indicating a significant increase in Indonesian fighting power, began to occur every time the Allied Forces stepped out of the Medan area.

REPATRIATION OF THE JAPANESE

In early January 1946, the first repatriation of Japanese from Sumatra was planned. Immediately after the surrender, we had guessed that it would take several years for Japanese marine transportation to reach us, because in Sumatra we were so far from Japan. However, repatriation was significantly speeded up when the American Liberty ships were offered for our use. In order to begin repatriation, our Imperial Guard Division wanted to prepare lodgings in Belawan, adjacent to the port, to permit the first group to gather.

However, Belawan was in terrible disorder due to the struggles and theft between the various independence parties who gathered there, hoping to get the goods that were being discharged in the port. Among these parties, the Fifth Corps was the most powerful because the corps had concentrated most of their power in Belawan where the greatest profit was expected. Pasukan Kelima, Pesindo, and the TKR struggled fiercely with each other, exchanging bullets every night. The police did not function at all. Even the military police in the TKR merely ran about. The whole of Belawan was very dangerous. On January 9, I received an order from the divisional headquarters to establish public peace in Belawan so that arrangements for the lodging for repatriation was possible.

In response to this divisional order, I first visited the intelligence unit of the Fifth Corps in order to find out what the real situation was like. "According to a report from the Japanese at Belawan Port, your Fifth Corps is making things very difficult for them. What is going on?" I asked.

The youths replied, "That is not true. The report must have been influenced by the other side's propaganda." In order to explain the position of the Fifth Corps in Belawan, a member of the intelligence unit, Pane, brought to me the next morning their Belawan branch director. The director was a tall, stout man. His sunburnt, copper-red face indicated his activity in Belawan. He sat in front of me politely and stressed the following: "Our Fifth Corps are making every possible effort to obtain independence. Consequently, it is very natural for us to be hated by the Allied Forces. But we have no intention of doing anything bad to the Japanese. It is very unexpected to gain the reputation that we are making things difficult for the Japanese. The Japanese who reported this to you were probably misinformed, hearing only from the one-sided Indonesians who oppose us."

I thought to myself that he may be right. A fair judgment is apt to be lost if information is taken from only one side of the two struggling with each other. However, I, myself, must be careful of doing the same thing, because I was now only receiving information from the Fifth Corps. Although this is what I thought, I answered, "Thank you. I am glad to hear that. However, if you exchange shots with the Allied Forces, or if you struggle with the Indonesians who oppose you, order will be disrupted in Belawan and it will be dangerous for the Japanese army to gather there for repatriation. We are simply afraid of the consequences. I understand the situation that you have explained, but I ask you to cooperate with us to establish order and safety."

THE BELAWAN CONFERENCE

Because I could roughly guess at the situation in Belawan, I visited Governor Hasan and asked him to make a plan to reestablish public peace there. Governor Hasan immediately summoned his staff to investigate the possibility. Because the government offices in Belawan had already almost stopped functioning, they decided to order the marshal of the Rabuhan police station, that was close to Belawan, to rule all of Belawan temporarily. Hasan explained to me, "He is a very able man. He is familiar with Belawan and very thoughtful as well. You can trust him because he is a strong-minded nationalist. You will have nothing to worry about, even if you are very frank with him."

I immediately agreed and they promptly took the appropriate steps. It was decided that the marshal would go with me to Belawan to try and settle things. I appreciated the ease of such diplomatic negotiation between trusting friends. While I was only agreeing and thanking them, without actually proposing anything from my side, everything was carried out just as I wished.

The next day, January 12, I went to the Rabuhan police station in a liaison office car with a green cross flag, accompanied by a member of Governor Hasan's staff to guide me. We arrived at the police station, after turning left halfway on the road to Belawan and then driving into the woods. The station was a two-story classic building with a rotunda in the center of the lawn. The red and white national flag of independent

Indonesia fluttered at the top of a pole in the front garden.

In the marshal's room, I found an unexpected visitor waiting for me. He was one of the youth leaders who had once visited me after the independence campaign had started in Tinjuwan Estate where I was spending a reclusive life farming. I recalled his clear and burning eyes when we discussed the future of the independence movement until late in the evening in the officers' dining room of my barracks. I shook his hand with the rapture of reunion. The marshal introduced him to me, "This is my eldest son."

The father and son in turn expressed their appreciation of my lasting goodwill towards Indonesian independence. We became friends immediately.

We went together to Belawan and called a meeting of delegates from the various parties at the city government office -- a two-story wooden building with an outside stairway, located close to the main road where the railroad to the port crossed it. The conference was held in a white-painted wooden building next to the office, roofed with old rusted zinc plates. The first floor was a vacant storage room. Climbing up a creaking stairway, I found the meeting room with simple long desks and benches that made it look like the classroom of a primary school.

Government Building and Conference Hall of Belawan City

In response to the call from the city government, all representatives from the various parties gathered quickly, for Belawan was a small city. The branch director of the Fifth Corps, who had come to me yesterday, took his seat, quietly greeting me. I sat on the side as an observer, and the marshal of the Rabuhan police station presided over the conference, inviting discussion over establishing public order. However, the delegates repeatedly blamed each other, and no conclusion appeared possible no matter how long the conference might continue. Finally I stood up, having lost my patience, and attempted to persuade them:

> Indonesia has proclaimed independence. The police is one of the government organs of the independent Indonesian Republic. The TKR is the national army of Indonesia. All parties that disturb the ability of these organs to perform their functions should be regarded as enemies of independence, regardless of their claims. In my position of having surrendered to the Allied Forces, I am not permitted to advise you about your independence. I am only asking you to establish peace and order in Belawan so as not to endanger the repatriation of the Japanese. I can only say that. However, if you claim that Indonesia is independent, you should be able to establish peace yourselves. If you say that you can't, the Japanese army will be obliged to do it. If you really want to achieve independence, you must support your governmental organs.

They didn't want the Japanese army ever to use their power again. Recalling the Tebing incident, all the delegates of the parties stopped arguing with each other and accepted my advice.

BELAWAN BECOMES SAFE AND PEACEFUL

Public peace was thus established in Belawan and no more reports of gunfire were heard thereafter. Lodging was safely arranged and Japanese soldiers and civilians began to concentrate in Belawan for the first repatriation.

I was thus able to fulfill the orders given by our division successfully. Such an establishment of order, however, restricted Fifth Corps activities. I felt deeply sorry that my action was driving my dear friends in the Fifth

Corps further into a corner, day by day. Although I was sorry, however, I could not help doing my best in my duty to secure the safety of the Japanese army.

The Belawan operation was the last occasion that I had business relations with the Fifth Corps. At the same time, it was probably also the last occasion that the Fifth Corps demonstrated significant power. The new commander of the corps, Dr. Nainggolan, had been almost completely disabled, suffering from severe psychasthenia since his imprisonment in Brastagi. The Fifth Corps' branch in Pangkalan Brandan was disbanded. In Binjai, 20 kilometers west of Medan, its branch had been weakened in a struggle with the Pesindo branch. Nervous about such a decline, Pane and others in the intelligence unit attempted to recover their relationship with Pesindo, as I had advised them, in order to reestablish the Fifth Corps as a section of Pesindo. However, the decline of the Fifth Corps continued.

CHAPTER SIXTEEN
LEAVING MEDAN

RESIGNATION FROM THE LIAISON OFFICE

One and a half months had passed since I took the job in the liaison office on December 1, 1945. The general situation had completely reversed itself during this period. The anti-Japanese trend in north Sumatra, which we had been so anxious about, had now completely ceased, and the mood of the Indonesian people had turned incredibly pro-Japanese. The Japanese, who had suffered all sorts of pain since surrendering, could now enjoy a safe life again, respected by the Indonesian people just like before the war ended. Consequently, I reported to my regiment commander that I had finished my duties of reestablishing friendship with the Indonesians by settling the Belawan affair, and asked him to advise the division commander to permit my resignation from the liaison office. I could thus return to my original company where my subordinates had missed me for one and a half months.

Dear Medan, I could hardly contain myself over my feelings of attachment to the work at the liaison office, which, though frightening, was worth the effort. However, in such work, the time to stop is very critical. If I were to continue, I would not know what would happen to me in the future. My current actions were thwarting NICA's strategies. If I were to continue for too long, there was a good possibility that I would be arrested and accused of war crimes by the Dutch. In a one-sided criminal trial, who could know by what distorted logic I could be convicted. Sensing the danger, I therefore sought a good opportunity to retire and I asked my regiment commander to withdraw me from my post. He kindly asked the division commander to permit me to withdraw, stressing that his regiment was keenly missing me as an important company commander and that Japanese-Indonesian relations had become so settled that my assistance was no longer needed.

Nevertheless, I could not help feeling deep emotion as I shook hands with Governor Hasan for the last time before departing. Medan was the second native place to which I had devoted my youth both before the war's end and again during this period. But I was obliged to leave the town. I had to return to the secluded life of farming in Tinjuwan, isolated from the history of the real world. It would be lonely, but otherwise I would be in danger.

SOANKUPON'S MUTTERING

Just before my leaving Medan, Maharaja Soankupon, the Republic's Resident assisting the governor, was sick in bed. I often visited his residence to inquire about him, but he was gradually worsening, sometimes getting a little better but then relapsing. He was already old and had a chronic disease called diabetes. The name of his current illness was obscure; it was sometimes said to be a gastroenteritis disorder and sometimes malaria. I brought him various drugs from the doctor's room at the liaison office, wanting to do all that I could for him, but he did not become better. He was already in a serious condition when I left Medan.

Maharaja Soankupon was always very kind to me. He was a very important person for us Japanese, having contributed to regaining the peace between Indonesians and Japanese. It was a great sadness for me to leave Medan with him seriously ill. On the day before my departure I visited his house, located on the west side of Raja Street. There was a garden in the front, and a porch leading to the drawing room where I had enjoyed many conversations with his family. The sick Soankupon was in a bed placed in a room on the left side of the garden.

Although he was very sick and barely conscious, he noticed me when his wife led me in. I took a chair placed close to him. His old and turbid eyes wet with tears, he extended his hand weakly from under the blanket and grasped my hand silently. He was on the brink of death before independence had been achieved. Looking at his old and haggard face, I was overcome by an unbearable grief. My fervent desire for his recovery ran deep in my heart. Mrs. Soankupon, who was watching us, finally began to weep uncontrollably.

After a short time, Soankupon, who was delirious with fever, suddenly opened his vacant eyes. Looking weakly at me, he muttered deliriously the name, "Mr. Fusali Rem," his brother-in-law, who was killed by mistake by the Japanese army in the Tebing incident. Taken unawares, I completely lost my presence of mind. In surprise, I wondered if he had not been convinced by my fictitious explanation that desperately tried to hide the truth. I wondered if his spirit, hovering on the border between life and death, had obtained some superhuman power to know the truth. I could not say anything because my throat was cramped. Maharaja Soankupon loved me like a blood-relative, and had endeavored, at the risk of his own old life, to cooperate with me to stop the conflict between the Japanese and Indonesians. I did not dare to reveal the truth to Soankupon that his brother-in-law had been killed by mistake by a Japanese soldier who was a close friend of mine, so I repeated the palliative explanation that he had been lost while entangled in the battle. Because Soankupon had stopped asking me about the incident and continued to receive me very kindly, I had felt somewhat relieved, thinking that he had been convinced. Now, however, I was afraid that his spirit had not been convinced. The words, "Mr. Fusali Rem," that he muttered looking at me, pierced my heart like a sword of ice. Soankupon soon fell asleep without waiting for my answer, but I could not stop my body trembling. Nirwan, who stood watching me trembling, offered me some comfort, "My father has gone off his head with the sickness. Please do not mind."

However, I could not forget Soankupon's face, as he fell asleep muttering in delirium, for a long time. The family of Imbalo were also there to enquire after Soankupon, for he was the uncle of Imbalo and Sahara. Sahara, who was usually very cheerful, saw me off quietly that day, giving me only a silent salutation.

FARMING AND READING AGAIN IN TINJUWAN

I left the liaison office in Medan on January 16 and returned to my dear communications company of the 4th Regiment that had been entrusted in my absence to the senior officer. Washing my hands of Indonesian affairs, I returned to my life of farming when it was clear, and reading when it rained. I returned to the position of a company commander in a defeated army.

The oil-palm trees of Tinjuwan, as always, were growing the rich dark green leaves under the tropical sunshine right over the equator. The vegetables that we had planted on the farm had grown surprisingly well in my absence and our daily meal was supplemented by the greens. The two soldiers whom I had sent to a Chinese bakery in Kisaran to study, were already back in our company having learnt to bake bread. They made a decorative cake to celebrate my return, using the British butter I brought back from the liaison office. My soldiers collected clams from the coast of Tanjung Tiram that had been the special place where we had initially landed. They made a kind of salted fish guts putting them in glass bottles. Master Sergeant Mori and others, who were expert hunters, hunted wild boar so deep into the woods that they were frightened by the footprints of tigers. Our whole company could enjoy sukiyaki with the meat.

The subsistence food was not the only thing that had improved. All the soldiers had become plump from getting enough rice. Five months ago when our regiment came to this estate from Aceh, after being crushed by the sorrowful surrender, many soldiers suffered from malnutrition which was apt to cause recurrent malaria, because we had to obey the staple food limitations imposed by the Allied Forces. A great amount of rice was, however, stored on this estate and the Indonesians willingly supplied the rice to the Japanese army. The supplement was outside the control of the Allied Forces.

In East Sumatra during Dutch colonialism, there were many estates producing a great deal of rubber, tobacco, and palm oil. But, rather than producing rice, they had imported it from Thailand or Burma, so the workers could not survive independently from the white managers. The Japanese army, when they occupied Sumatra, switched the greater part of the estates to rice cultivation in order to establish an independent food supply. This agricultural policy of the Japanese military government was now enabling the Indonesian people to fight for independence without worrying about food. Therefore, the Indonesian farmers, who were once more pro-Japanese, had no objection to supplying rice to the Japanese. The improvement in Japanese-Indonesian relations thus affected everything.

On the other hand, the Domei News Service was reporting that the Japanese in our fatherland were starving and eating the runners of potatoes or bean cake. Some of them were dying of hunger. We were full of sympathy for our compatriots starving in our fatherland, comparing their hardships to our situation in Sumatra. I always encouraged the improvement of our diets even beyond traditional army standards, in order to send back healthy young soldiers for the economic reconstruction of Japan. I found out now, that in my absence, that effort was yielding fruit. During my absence, the senior officer, 1st Lt. Kamiya, who was commanding my company for me, had been called to the port of Belawan as an interpreter and so the youngest officer, 2nd Lt. Osada was in charge of the company until I returned. Although Osada was a very new officer, who had recently been promoted from regular soldier, my company had maintained excellent order and unity and welcomed my return cheerfully. My dear staff each reported to me the various things that had happened in the regiment during my absence. Listening to their reports, I had a very pleasant meal with them, and was filled with a sense of nostalgia.

Anyway, my company was my home, where I could be most relaxed. In Medan I could not be free from tension, even for a moment, because I bore the destiny of 20,000 Japanese in Sumatra on my shoulders. Here, I was literally revived. My company was my home.

SOANKUPON'S DEATH

One month after I returned to the seclusion of life in Tinjuwan, a letter reached me from the liaison office in Medan. It informed me of the death of Soankupon. The thing I was afraid of had happened. I was greatly shocked and left speechless for a while.

Many memories of Soankupon one by one appeared on the back screen of my closed eyelids like pictures from a revolving lantern: his home on the west side of Raja Street, where he lived with his wife, his elder son, Nirwan, and his younger daughter. When I visited his home, his old body tottered out to the drawing room and, delighted, he would ask me to take a seat. He explained various aspects of Batak folklore in rapid and elegant Indonesian. He waved his hand to me like a young girl when he saw me riding a bicycle along the street. When the Tebing incident occurred, he chaired the meeting of representatives from the various parties. He had resolutely looked around the young fighters and asked: "Dear Comrades. Do you really want to make the Japanese the enemy?"

I could not help feeling as lonely as if I had lost my own father. However, I did not cry but held back my tears. I was a man who did not cry, even when Japan surrendered. I held the letter silently and stared at a corner of the ceiling until a knock sounded on the door.

THE FAMILY PLAYED WITH BY FATE

In the last part of February, our 4th Imperial Guard Infantry Regiment was ordered to move to Pangkalan Brandan because the air-guard regiment that had been staying there was leaving Sumatra as the second group to be repatriated. On the way to Brandan, I stopped my truck in Raja Street, in Medan. In Soankupon's house, Nirwan was living alone dejectedly. I first expressed my sympathy for the death of his father. I then asked about the Fifth Corps. Their headquarters in Medan had already collapsed and the branch director in Tebing Tinggi, Parapat, was the new commander for the Fifth Corps in the province. Nirwan told me, "Our Fifth Corps has gone completely to ruin. After you left Medan, our commander, Dr. Nainggolan, was arrested twice by the Indonesians and then arrested a third time by the Dutch army and was hidden somewhere. The situation is inexpressibly bad."

I thus found out that Dr. Nainggolan had finally been taken by the Dutch army. Did they arrest him for the guerrilla activities that he directed? But then, the people in the street believed that he was protected by the Dutch. Was he really protected as rumored? Or, did the Dutch take him by force, seizing an opportunity when he was cornered, in order to use him for their own purposes? Was he really, as rumored, an agent of NICA? Did he willingly escape into the Dutch army? Or, though he himself was a real freedom fighter, he might have unwillingly fled to the Dutch army because he was falsely accused of being a traitor by the Indonesians. Fate had dealt him a curious hand. What was the truth? I could not make a decisive judgment. A Japanese said to me, boasting of his correct judgment, "You remember? I warned you to be careful of him. It is now clear that, as I warned you, he was an agent of NICA."

However, I still liked to think of him as one of the real freedom fighters. He was the father of Bob and Boyke, whom I heartily loved and believed in. A man is apt to make a clear-cut judgement arbitrarily and conclude that something is this way or that. However, nothing can be ultimately clarified. The real mind of a person is sometimes unknown, even to himself. Who has the right to say arrogantly that he knows the mind of another person? Is it possible to know the real truth in this world when complicated human psychology is involved? History often advances promptly to the next page after leaving an arbitrary judgement not much concerned with the real truth. Whatever the truth may be, Dr. Nainggolan was placed among a group of Indonesians who lost their fatherland by being branded as agents of NICA.

How sad it was for the sons of Dr. Nainggolan. Where were the hot-blooded Bob and Boyke who had been fighting for independence, persistently believing in their father and Sihite? Did they pursue independence, abandoning their father, or did they follow their father and abandon independence? Even if they pursued independence, could they be accepted by the people who suspected them? The family of Nainggolan, who were being played with by fate, were thus coming to a sad and mysterious end, together with Sihite, who had also tried to play with fate.

JUSUF is KILLED IN A GUERRILLA ATTACK

I also wondered about Ismed, who was most intimate and friendly with me, and always cheerfully fought in the independence war. Nirwan knew about him very well because Ismed was his cousin. He told me that he was back in Siantar staying with his father. Because he was always so optimistic and active, I felt sure that he would be planning something or another. He was a cheerful fighter who never lost his optimism. I was not too anxious about him because I believed that he would live cleverly, switching his mind to new things, regardless of the situation.

The one for whom I was most anxious was Jusuf. With a faded cap on his head, wearing a scruffy white shirt, he was suffering from the dilemma of choosing between independence and love. He was the one most afraid of having me doubt his patriotism and would often come to ask me "Do you believe me?"

How was Jusuf doing after I left Medan, I wondered, because a friend of mine who remained in the liaison office told me recently, "I have seen Jusuf occasionally in the RAPWI camp. He seems to have finally joined the RAPWI as a traitor, overcome by the charm of a girl."

However, I never wanted to believe it. Even supposing that he was following his lover, Merry, I could not be sure of his personal happiness.

Even if he wanted to follow his lover and abandon his father, his home, and fatherland, would Merry welcome him? Even if Merry herself wanted to welcome him, would her family agree to have him, a Batak, accompany them back to the Netherlands as her husband? Even if he did marry her, could he be happy for long? While I was wondering this, I became caught up in an illusion, as if Jusuf had really gone to the Netherlands, and I muttered a silent prayer, "Miss Merry, Jusuf is a weak man. Please love him forever and do not abandon him."

Even with Nirwan here, I hesitated to ask about Jusuf because I was afraid of the truth. Nevertheless, I could not help asking because I was so anxious about him. The story that Nirwan told me was very surprising -- Jusuf had been killed during a guerrilla attack. The morning after a night attack in early February, he was found alone, lying dead among some coconut trees, wet with the morning dew.

Alone in my room in the new barracks in Pangkalan Brandan, I thought back to the story I had heard from Nirwan and secretly offered my tears to Jusuf who died alone, but as a respectable patriot. I bowed to him saying in my heart, "Dear Jusuf. You were a glorious patriot. You were a splendid freedom fighter. I am sorry that I doubted you. I believe you now. Please believe that I believe you now."

Jusuf was a weak man. However, all Indonesians, both weak and strong, were devoting their lives to independence. This was the strength of the independence movement. The desire for merdeka was burning in the hearts of all hundred million Indonesians.

CHAPTER SEVENTEEN
HOPING FOR INDONESIAN SUCCESS

THE PEOPLE'S FRONT COUP D'ETAT

After I resigned from the liaison office and returned to my home regiment, the independence movement in Sumatra continued, creating stories more checkered than any found in novels. Initially after the Tebing Tinggi incident, the people in Sumatra enjoyed significantly improved public order. However, some rumors began to circulate, telling how some Sultans and Rajas, who were used to enjoying a luxurious life under the protection of the Dutch, were now starting to become pro-Dutch again. I was secretly afraid that my efforts of goodwill since the Tebing incident might have harmed Indonesian independence.

However, something surprising happened. It was the dawn of March 2, soon after I moved to Pangkalan Brandan. A coup d'etat suddenly occurred throughout the whole of East Sumatra Province and the traditional ruling class was completely overthrown. The various independence parties, who had thus far been divided and struggling with each other, had organized, unnoticed, a people's union for cooperation. After secret preparations, they simultaneously attacked the ruling classes throughout East Sumatra. Some were killed and most were arrested. They were confined in two camps in Kabanjahe and Pematang Siantar, with males and females separated. I admired the dexterous operation.

Regardless of the coup d'etat, the position of the governor of Sumatra, Hasan, was not shaken. But, Resident Tengku Hafas, who was a relative of the Sultan of Deli, lost his position, and Yunus Nasution, a Batak and one of the Communist leaders, became the Resident of East Sumatra Province. The general commander of the coup d'etat was Dr. Gindo Siregar of the Communist party. He carried it out with the support of Abdul Xarim, the commander of the PKI in Sumatra.

When the Japanese military government lost actual power with their surrender, Xarim quickly brought a few rubber estates under his control and established a fund by selling the rubber to junks coming from Malaya. He was thus waiting for an opportunity, conserving his power by feeding his soldiers and buying arms. In contrast to the Communists in Java, he was always sympathetic to the Japanese. When the Tebing incident occurred, only the TKR and the Communist party commanded by Xarim did not join in the attack on the Japanese. The Communist party steadily extended its power by not becoming involved in the various struggles. They were thus finally able to triumph and grasp the leadership of the whole freedom fight.

After this coup d'etat, a newspaper reported that the office of the East Sumatran Provincial Resident was located in Binjai City, 20 kilometers west of Medan. Even though I had already retired from the liaison office, I was very interested in the political situation, since it was changing in ways we hadn't predicted. One day I dropped in at the new office to see the new Resident on my way back from Medan. I was always welcomed by Indonesians because I was known as a friendly, Indonesian-speaking Japanese officer. The new Resident, Yunus, welcomed me with a bright smile and talked with pride about his ambitious plans.

A: Amir Syarifudin, Minister of Defense of RI
T: Colonel A. Tahir, Division Commander of TRI
S: Lt. Colonel Sucipto, Division Chief Staff Officer of TRI in Pematang Siantar, 1946

However, a week later when I visited the office again, another person received me. To my surprise, Yunus had been arrested by Pesindo and was being held in the Binjai prison. In astonishment, I questioned why. The new Resident explained that Yunus appointed only his relatives and Communists to important positions and earned money for his family and party by abusing his control over economic matters. The new Resident was Luat Siregar, a Batak also, but supported by the youth party.

Although I was no longer a member of the liaison office, I always enjoyed hearing various items of information from my friends there. So I often visited them in Medan. I drove the 120 kilometers between Medan and Pangkalan Brandan alone on a motorcycle, but there was no danger. The Indonesian sentries guarding various spots saluted me with their rifles or spears because I was an officer in the army of a friend of Indonesia.

READYING FOR THE DECISIVE BATTLE

Governor Hasan moved the government of Sumatra inland, to Pematang Siantar, not wanting to stay in Medan where the Allied Forces were. The national army, the TKR, changed its name to TRI (Indonesian Republican Forces) and prohibited the other parties from calling themselves *tentera* (army or forces). The first class graduated from the military academy that was founded in the Karo Highlands, and the national army was steadily replenished. The TRI was proud of its disciplined order and sense of unity under the command of Col. Tahir, a wise man of excellent personality and previously a lieutenant in the volunteer Indonesian army trained by the Japanese. Pesindo, that used to clash with the TKR, began to cooperate with the national army, to prepare for the coming decisive battle against the Dutch.

As the repatriation of the Japanese progressed, the Japanese army was beginning to concentrate in the Medan area, as troops were withdrawn from more distant places. In May, the 25th Army Headquarters, which had been located in Bukit Tinggi in West Sumatra, moved to Binjai. Following the retiring Japanese army, the Indonesian troops moved their front forward, adjacent to the Japanese front, surrounding the Medan-Binjai area.

A SECRET PRESENT OF ARMS

Immediately after the war's end, we, the Japanese soldiers, were quite pessimistic about repatriation. We were afraid that we would be detained in Sumatra for our whole lives, working to reconstruct things damaged by the war. But when we observed the reality of the third group gathering in Belawan for repatriation, our hopes for the future began to brighten. At the same time, our desire increased day by day to leave something to the Indonesian people, who were preparing for a decisive battle with the Dutch army. Secret connections between the Japanese and Indonesian armies began to be established in many places. Most Japanese troops had omitted some of their arms from the list submitted to the Allied Forces to cover an emergency. These surplus arms were little by little reaching the Indonesians. Most of us had no earnest desire to prevent the flow of arms. The Tebing Tinggi massacre had disrupted it for a while, but once Japanese-Indonesian friendship was restored the flow continued, and even increased, so as to get rid of the excess arms before leaving Sumatra.

For example, the Indonesian troops who formed a front in the farming area south of Binjai, would often make night attacks after informing the Japanese troops beforehand. When gun shots sounded in the night sky, the Japanese troops would go out and shoot into the air to make a lot of noise. Then they would retire leaving many boxes of bullets in a predetermined place. The Indonesians would gratefully pick them up. The sounds must have been picked up by the Allied Forces either directly or through their emissaries. The Japanese troops, however, would report this as a battle in which many bullets were consumed in an attempt to repulse a night attack by Indonesian forces. Consequently, any history relying on formal records can never be accurate.

When the 2nd Battalion of the 3rd Infantry Regiment left Kabanjahe for repatriation, many rifles and machine guns were left under the floor. Japanese deserters had been secretly informed beforehand so that Indonesian troops guided by the deserters found them immediately. Because presents to Indonesians were always left behind when Japanese troops departed from their barracks, the Indonesians competed in their attempts to communicate with the Japanese that they knew. The presents were not only arms but also various other kinds of military goods. The majority of the goods stored by the Japanese Field Storehouse were given to the TRI in exchange for a guarantee of security for the Japanese being repatriated.

RESCUE OF SUSPECTED WAR CRIMINALS

In early July, our 4th Regiment finally received repatriation orders and moved to Belawan from Pangkalan Brandan.

In Belawan, the Allied Forces carried out war criminal checks, summoning several people including officers from each company. Two examiners interviewed the officers, questioning them in various ways. Because the war criminal trials at that time were decided at the first hearing, there was no chance to make a counter-argument once someone was accused in a one-sided trial. The Allied Forces, particularly the Dutch, who had lost Sumatra in the Japanese southern advance, were thought to be keen to retaliate by finding some scapegoat among the defeated soldiers facing them. Consequently, we could not help trembling before the examiners, feeling we were trapped in a maze that led to a guillotine. Fortunately, however, I passed the examination together with my subordinates. The interrogation actually seemed to me to be surprisingly fair. One of the examiners was Captain Follan who spoke beautiful Japanese. He had reputedly been born to a Japanese mother in Singapore, but that was not true. He had actually been one of the language students specially trained in Japanese in London during the war for posting to the Asian front. Even the Dutch examiner who bore a grudge against the Japanese could not move too far under the supervision of the British who bore no direct grudge against the Japanese in Sumatra.

However, such a fortunate outcome was not shared by all. Five officers of the 3rd Machine Gun Company were suspected and imprisoned in the Black Camp for prisoners undergoing trial. They had repeated the same answer, "I have forgotten," to all the questions they were asked. This was a peculiar custom in the Japanese army where a soldier would use it to excuse himself when he could not answer a senior officer's question. The officer would scold him if he said he didn't know, but would not if he said he had forgotten. This funny, traditional custom was unfortunately not considered so by the foreign army. Instead, the officers were suspected of hiding something. Our regiment commander was very anxious about them because he was afraid that they would be made material for Dutch retaliation if they were left behind in a prison. So he ordered me to rescue them.

I went to the very familiar liaison office. A liaison officer managing Allied Forces' affairs called the examiners to the liaison office to see me. When they came, I explained the purpose of the meeting: "We are extremely happy that our regiment can be repatriated after passing your very fair examination. Please accept these small gifts in gratitude from us."

Saying this, I presented them with a few gifts. The examiners accepted them with thanks and said, "Congratulations on your repatriation. We wish you a happy journey."

After the gifts had been accepted, I said, "We do have one problem. Five of our officers are in the Black Camp on suspicion. Although I am afraid it may be difficult for you to understand, their replies conformed to a traditional format used in the Japanese army. If you would examine them further, I am sure that you will find them innocent. Please could you interrogate them again as soon as possible so that they can be repatriated with us."

They agreed to reexamine them. Breathlessly, I waited for the reaction from the Allied Forces. After two days a message arrived asking me to go to the Black Camp to receive the officers, who were being released. Dancing for joy, I went by truck to the dreadful Black Camp, that was located in Gelugur Village midway along the road to Belawan. It was surrounded by a concrete wall over 3 meters high, topped with a barbed wire fence. The gate was guarded by Dutch and Indian soldiers holding rifles with bayonets. Leaving my truck outside the gate, I entered the camp. When the heavy iron door closed behind me with a thud, I trembled, thinking that I might not come back out because I was a man who had frustrated one Dutch strategy after another when I was in the liaison office. I could not help expecting to be told, "You yourself are a war criminal. You, too, must stay here."

Escorted by a British officer who was expecting me, I came to a cell in the prison. The five Japanese officers were sitting or lying on the wet concrete floor in only their underwear, with all their other clothes taken. I quickly asked for their clothes to be returned so we could get back outside the iron gate. One of them claimed that their watches and fountain pens had been taken, but I shouted at them, "Don't be silly. Your lives are more important than your watches. Hurry up!"

I ordered my driver to start the truck immediately. But, looking back at the iron gate being closed once again with a thud, I could not help grieving for the other Japanese prisoners who remained helpless there, because I had only rescued the five people in our regiment.

No GRUDGE AGAINST THE DUTCH

While I was busy with such affairs, my subordinates were mustered for the loading and unloading of vessels in Belawan Harbor, and were experiencing the misery of being the defeated enemy for the first time. The Dutch soldiers had a grudge against the Japanese for taking Sumatra. They faced the Japanese as the victors and forced my subordinates to work, wielding whips and using angry voices filled with hatred. My subordinates reported to me angrily of their rough treatment from Dutch soldiers when they were back in their temporary barracks.

Belawan Harbor   T.F.

I, however, could not feel a grudge against the Dutch, even after hearing such reports. A Dutch repatriation ship lay at anchor in the Belawan port. Many Dutch colonists born in Sumatra were boarding the ship with only the clothes that they were wearing. They were being repatriated to a fatherland that they had never seen. I knew that they had spent three and a half years as prisoners in the camp controlled by the Japanese army. I could guess at how hard and sorrowful that life was for them. Although Japan had been defeated and they were rescued by the advancing Allied Forces, they could no longer live here safely as before the war, because Indonesia had raised the flag of independence. Regardless of the fact that they were the victors, they had lost all the property they had accumulated here over many years, and were obliged to leave Sumatra where they had been born.

While they looked sternly at the Japanese soldiers, their powerless figures climbing the ladder to the repatriation ship could only invoke pity. Although they were colonial aggressors, the Japanese advance had frustrated them of the fruits of their exploitation, which I am sure they felt also contributed to Sumatra's development. I was deeply sympathetic towards them, with some feelings of remorse.

THE KIND INDIAN SOLDIERS

In contrast to the Dutch, the Indian soldiers in Belawan were very kind to the Japanese. The British-Indian forces that advanced to Sumatra were the same troops who had fought against the Japanese in Burma. Indian officers told us that their force of one regiment could not advance for one whole day because of a bridge that was defended by only a few Japanese soldiers. They paid us unexpected respect, even though we were defeated, praising the Japanese soldiers as the world's strongest fighters.

When the Japanese soldiers were working under the supervision of the British-Indian army, Indian soldiers often ordered them to rest in the shade and served them various types of food. They ordered the Japanese soldiers to finish up their daily work earlier, and gave them a lot of canned foods, saying: "Our India is also becoming independent soon. When we are independent, let us cooperate as brother nations."

On the day before our boarding, I received another order from our regiment commander. In accordance with his order, I visited the port commander of the British-Indian army with a Japanese sword as a gift. The commander was an Indian major. He was of a noble family from the Kashmir district and his orderly was a servant from his castle there. I conveyed to him the request from our regiment commander:

> We have already sent two groups for repatriation. You are examining the property of the repatriating soldiers at the harbor. But, it seems that the examiners often take valuable or attractive goods even though the Japanese have only goods within the permitted limits. Because the Japanese in Japan are now suffering from a shortage of food and all kinds of goods, we would like to bring to Japan as much as we can within the limits. Please ask your examiners not to take such things.

The port commander willingly agreed. In addition, he permitted the loading of surplus rice on our ship and proposed giving us a large amount of soap and tobacco that they had seized from Japanese field storage, to help the hungry people in Japan.

He served us an Indian curry that, though very delicious, was too hot for us. We had a happy conversation for a while, discussing the future of India and Japan. He asked me to give him my home address in Japan because he wanted to send me some Kashmir cloth in return for the sword when he returned to his home country. I politely declined by explaining that I did not know yet where I would be living because of the air-raid bombing. In reality, I was afraid that leaving my address here might enable my later arrest as a war criminal who had incited independence for Indonesia or India. I was probably silly to be so nervous but we were so afraid at that time of the war crimes trials ignoring the basic principles of law.

HOPING FOR THE SUCCESS OF INDONESIAN INDEPENDENCE

After spending a week in Belawan, we boarded the repatriation ship on July 14, 1946. The ship was a 5,000-ton freighter of the Liberty Type, offered by the Americans for our repatriation.

Because our living area, which had been made by fixing a wooden floor over the hatch and placing mats on it, was unbearably warm during the day, we all enjoyed the cooler air on deck. Our ship full of half-naked Japanese soldiers sailed to the east, rolling slightly on the Straits of Malacca, known for their clean and calm water. In the far distance to the south, the smoking volcano of Mt. Sibayak in the violet haze of the Karo Highlands overlooked the Medan plains and our ship on the Malacca Straits. Continuing to look back at Sumatra where I had spent four and a half years of my youth, I extended my thoughts to the future of the independence movement and to the Indonesians who were living and fighting there.

The wireless news received on the ship reported current events in the world. The Americans, who had destroyed our desire to liberate Asia by defeating us at the head of the Allied Forces, unexpectedly recognized Philippine independence that had been granted by the Japanese, and supported, in an international conference, Indonesian independence. Before boarding this ship, we had heard from the Indonesians the unbelievable news that some American commercial ships were selling arms to the Indonesians after passing through the Dutch Navy blockade.

On the other hand, even the British, who were cooperating with the Dutch, had promised India independence and were preparing for it. The British also seemed intent on recognizing the independence of Burma that had been granted by the Japanese. Although Japan had lost the liberation war, the dream of Asian liberation seemed to be becoming a reality.

Such international trends made my heart flutter, suggesting the possibility of success for Indonesian independence. We heard that the British forces were leaving Indonesia once Japanese repatriation had been completed. How would my beloved Indonesian youths fight against the Dutch after the British and Japanese withdrawal?

Our ship turned north after stopping over one day in Singapore. Crossing several thousands of kilometers of waves, we arrived in Ujina Port, and stepped on the earth of the fatherland that I had missed for six years, where my parents and brothers lived. In our occupied country, where all industries had been destroyed by airraid bombing, the Japanese people were fighting bitterly against hunger. Therefore, I also was forced to join in the fight against hunger. Nevertheless, I continued to pray for the success of Indonesian independence, thinking of my friends in the southern country whom I was not sure I would ever see again.

CHAPTER EIGHTEEN
INDONESIA AFTER MY REPATRIATION

THE INDEPENDENCE WAR AFTER OUR REPATRIATION

Repatriation of the Japanese from Sumatra was completed in October 1946. The British-Indian army withdrew from Sumatra in November. The Dutch army, thus unconfined, carried out the so-called first police action (or first aggression as it is called by the Indonesians) to recover their former territory in one stroke. The Indonesian troops around the Medan area counter-attacked against the Dutch forces and tried to frustrate their actions. This counterattack was launched simultaneously in many places, including Java. The Indonesian army continued their resistance, repeating their strategy of advance and retreat. The solidarity between the various resistance forces in Indonesia was considerably tightened as a result of these battles. At the same time, they began to appeal to world public opinion by presenting their case to the United Nations.

In response to this diplomatic offensive, the Dutch tried to avoid blame by proposing Indonesian independence within a framework of federal states under Dutch suzerainty. At the same time, they intended to retain substantial control by planning the establishment of small puppet states to divide Indonesia. In the Medan area, a puppet state called *Negara Sumatra Timur* (the country of East Sumatra) was established and Dr. Mansur, a medical doctor who used to be the director of the Medan City Hospital and was married to a Dutch woman, was appointed as *wali* (governor). Reinforced by new soldiers trained in Canada with modern arms, the Dutch gradually extended their occupied area, approaching the foot of the Karo Highlands. In Java, Indonesian forces continued to resist, moving the Indonesian central government inland, from Jakarta to Yogyakarta.

During this unstable midway point of the independence war, the Indonesian Communist Party, in September 1948, suddenly took off its veil and rebelled against the Republic of Indonesia led by Sukarno and Hatta. The Communists, dreaming of independence within world communism, finally disclosed their real aim. They occupied the city of Madiun in a coup d'etat, and proclaimed the establishment of a Communist government. Sukarno called on the people by radio to choose between the two, and was able to overcome the crisis by defeating the Communist army with the support of the majority of the people.

Taking advantage of this confusion, the Dutch launched the so-called second police action (or aggression) in December 1948. In Sumatra they occupied the whole plain of East Sumatra Province from Tanjung Balai in the east to Tanjung Pura in the west, and advanced further, occupying all the cities in the Karo and Tapanuli Highlands by dropping paratroopers. In Java, Dutch paratroopers captured President Sukarno and Vice-President Hatta in a sudden attack on Yogyakarta, the capital of the Indonesian Republic, and confined them initially in Parapat, a resort town by Lake Toba, in Sumatra, and later on the island of Bangka.

INDEPENDENCE IS FINALLY COMPLETED

Although all the important cities and areas were occupied by the Dutch, and the president and vice-president captured, the Indonesians kept the Republic functioning by establishing an emergency government in central Sumatra. Aceh itself remained independent and formed an important part of the emergency government, because the Dutch did not dare enter this province since it was well defended by the strong Acehnese forces. Hearing this news in Japan, I was secretly proud that I had prevented these Acehnese forces from being destroyed in a clash with the Japanese army, by cooperating with Governor Hasan in 1945.

The author in front of the lakeside villa in Parapat where
Sukarno and Hatta were imprisoned at the end of 1948

The Indonesian forces in other provinces also continued their resistance through scorched-earth tactics. In East Sumatra, they burnt out the highland cities such as Kabanjahe and Brastagi, and completely destroyed the oil refinery in Pangkalan Brandan that was eagerly coveted by the Dutch. They destroyed small outposts of the Dutch army by siege. They smuggled agitators into the cities. The Dutch army was thus gradually driven back into a defensive position.

At the same time, the provisional Indonesian government strengthened its astute diplomatic offensive by flying the first Indonesian airline from Kota Raja in Aceh to New Delhi in India. Public opinion in the United States became increasingly sympathetic to Indonesia. The British who were ready to permit Indian independence, also became sympathetic towards Indonesia. The number of countries supporting Indonesian independence increased day by day, and the Netherlands became surrounded by foes. In June 1949, the Dutch released Sukarno and Hatta, and bitterly agreed to recognize Indonesian independence at a Round Table Conference in The Hague in August. On December 27, 1949, Indonesia formally completed the independence process, and Indonesians thus stepped into a glorious new era.

A FIRST VISIT TO DEAR SUMATRA

Japan also stepped into a new era as a peace-loving nation. The Japanese soldiers who spent their youth in Sumatra during the war were now more than 50 years old. They became old enough to enjoy nostalgia and began to take nostalgic trips. Consequently, in 1972 the veterans from the communications company of the 4th Imperial Guard Infantry Regiment, that I used to command, organized a tourist group of around seventy, together with the veterans from the Independent Heavy Artillery Battalion that had been stationed nearby, to visit Aceh, which they had once defended. Because I was too busy to join the tour, I attended the war comrades meeting afterwards to hear about the trip. I felt unspeakable emotion when they described their experiences and showed slides and movies they had taken in Sumatra. When they landed at Bulan Bintang Airport in Banda Aceh (what used to be Kota Raja), the Acehnese governor, accompanied by many of his staff, held a welcoming ceremony presenting the visitors with leis. Because there was no commercial sightseeing bus, the Indonesian air force offered two military buses with drivers for the Japanese to use during their stay. Two female students from the English college served as guides.

Visiting the towns and villages that they had once defended, the tour group was enthusiastically welcomed by the Acehnese. The inhabitants of Sigli welcomed them with a folk dance. In the village of Raueun, the village head, who had been a small boy during the war, cried, embarrassing a Japanese veteran when he recalled his memories of the soldier. Hearing these reports, I felt an unspeakable contentment that the love between the Japanese and Indonesians that I had experienced in my youth had been confirmed. The brotherhood I had felt at that time was no illusion.

In 1974, I got the chance to visit Sumatra personally. When I attended the Asian Pacific Dental Congress in Jakarta, representing Japan, I extended my trip to dear Sumatra. When my plane from Jakarta flew over the east end of East Sumatra, the great falls of Asahan, surrounded by green, appeared clearly on the mountainside of the Tapanuli Highlands. It had been reported that Southeast Asia's largest power station was being constructed here with Japanese aid. In the highlands above the falls, the surface of Lake Toba, the holy birth place of the Batak people, was shining brilliantly. The plane then flew over the city of Tebing Tinggi, where for me the memory of the riots was unforgettable. In the jungle along the seashore close to the town, an aluminum refining factory, the largest in the Orient, was being constructed using the electric power from the Asahan Falls. A harbor was also being planned nearby. Dear Tebing was thus rapidly becoming a modern city. My plane finally reached Medan. When I saw that Mt. Sibayak was still smoking on the front ridge of the Karo Highlands, hiding the immortal fire and a scene I used to see daily, I became crazy with joy.

In Medan, where I landed after an absence of nearly thirty years, the population had expanded from 160,000 to 600,000, but the condition of the old town quarters, where I had lived, showed almost no change. Through a travel agency owned by a Japanese deserter, I hired a taxi and renewed the memories of my youth by visiting one by one all the dear places where I had run around risking my life. I became increasingly delighted on finding the Indonesian people everywhere as friendly as I had experienced thirty years previously. I took meals in small roadside restaurants rather than in the large hotel restaurants, in order to taste the pure Indonesian food.

THE FATE OF ONE FAMILY

Of course, I tried to find out about my dear friends with whom I had had no communication since I was repatriated from Sumatra. Although I saw no change in Governor Hasan's house when I visited -- even in the lawns and tropical trees -- the people living there were completely different. I was told that Governor Hasan, who moved to Java after becoming a member of Parliament when independence was achieved, was now enjoying a quiet life in Jakarta. All of my other elderly friends had passed away. Most of the youths in the intelligence unit, who were very close to me, no longer lived in Medan having assumed more important positions in Java. The chief of the intelligence unit of the Fifth Corps, Nirwan Siregar, was said to be a government officer in Kalimantan.

A Japanese deserter who was now an Indonesian citizen told me of the extraordinary, checkered history of the the Nainggolan family whose lives continued to be played with by fate. It was really dramatic, far beyond my imagination. Although I did not know at that time, the mother and sister of Bob and Boyke were killed by Pesindo in Brastagi during the coup d'etat by the People's Front. During the Dutch period, the mother and sister had enjoyed the Dutch lifestyle, and often rode horses around Brastagi in the Karo Highlands wearing colorful riding suits. When the coup d'etat was planned, Dr. Nainggolan was already under arrest by the Dutch army, though in reality he was reputedly under their protection. Therefore, it was no wonder that the Pesindo youths would think them dangerous and kill them. Hearing such a sorrowful story thirty years later, I felt very sad for my dear old friend, Boyke, imagining how hard he would have taken such news.

A group of freedom fighters' leaders meeting in Kota Raja (Banda Aceh) in 1948. At the left of the front line (marked with an X) is Captain Boyke Nainggolan. In the center of the back line (marked with an N) is Major Nip Xarim, Battalion Commander

The manly Boyke did not abandon his fatherland, even when he was persecuted in this way. When the Dutch army launched the first police action (aggression) after the Japanese and British armies had left Sumatra, Boyke -- originally an officer in the volunteer Indonesian army trained by the Japanese -- joined the national army, commanded troops, and, facing Dutch aggression, did not permit the enemy to advance.

However, fate gave him another merciless blow. His father, Dr. Nainggolan, was appointed as the minister of health in the puppet government of the State of East Sumatra established by the Dutch. This confirmed that he was an agent of NICA. Nevertheless, the freedom fighter, Boyke, was not deterred and continued to fight against the pro-Dutch government of which his father was a part. However, the Indonesian army was gradually driven back and most of his comrades retreated into the Karo Highlands. Boyke, however, did not want to go to the Karo Highlands because that was the place where his mother and sister had been cruelly killed.

He fled alone to Aceh but soon returned to East Sumatra and hid himself in Tebing Tinggi. Then, the second police action was undertaken by the Dutch in December 1948. The Dutch army occupied Tebing City in a sudden attack and captured Boyke. I did not hear the details of how he met his father when he was brought to Medan. His father arranged for him to be sent to the Netherlands to study at the military academy of Breda.

When Indonesia achieved independence from the Dutch in 1949, the puppet state was absorbed peacefully by the Indonesian Republic. Dr. Nainggolan returned to being a medical doctor, having lost all his public positions. Boyke returned to Medan after graduating from the Dutch military academy and was appointed an officer in the Indonesian National Army. Col. Simbolon, the commander of his military district, highly appreciated Boyke's ability and appointed him commander of the Medan Guard Battalion.

However, Boyke seems to have been born under a really mysterious star. His fate became entangled in another stormy event. In December 1956, seven years after he returned to Medan, his respected senior, Col. Simbolon, proclaimed self-government for North Sumatra, protesting against the pro-Communist and centralization policies of Sukarno, and entrenched his troops in the mountains of Tapanuli. In March of the next year, he officially rebelled against the central government by establishing the Indonesian Republic Revolutionary Government (PRRI) in concert with like-minded groups in West Sumatra and Aceh. When his senior left Medan, Boyke was promoted to deputy commander of the government army in Medan because he pretended to have nothing to do with the rebellion. But, when Simbolon proclaimed the new government, he suddenly changed. Mobilizing all the troops under his control, he occupied all the transportation and communication facilities in the area and joined the rebellion.

In response to the rebellion, the central government mobilized the three forces -- army, navy, and air force -- and seized back the Medan area by dropping paratroopers on Polonia airport in Medan, and sending an overwhelming army through Belawan port. The defeated Boyke fled far into the mountains of Tapanuli to join Col. Simbolon. The incident was reported briefly in the Japanese newspapers. At the time, when I had read the name Nainggolan, I had wondered anxiously if the rebel might be Boyke Nainggolan. Coming here now, I discovered that it was.

The author (standing) with his dear friend and former freedom fighter Ismed in 1979 after losing contact for 33 years. Ismed was incidentally the industrial attaché of the Indonesian Embassy in Tokyo. He became later President of a Bank and then a National congressman, but passed away in 1989.

The author (right) with his dear friend the freedom fighter Nirwan in Jakarta in 1990 after losing contact for 44 years. Nirwan recently retired from government service in Kalimantan.

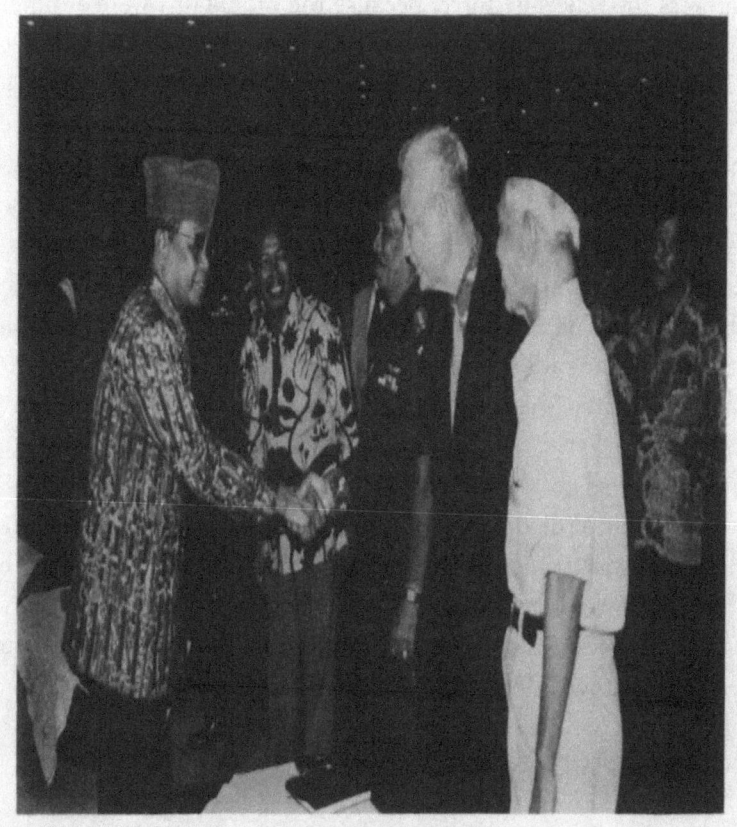

Col. A. Tahir, Division Commander of TKR in Medan during the Liberation War is now a General, Past Minister of Communications, and President of the Indonesian Veterans Association. When the author visited Indonesia in 1990, he was invited as a guest to the Veterans Conference held in Medan and shook hands with Gen. Tahir. The person standing on the right is Mr. Nip Xarim, Chairman of the Freedom Fighter Veterans Council in the Medan Area.

Even the government forces with their overwhelming power could not suppress the rebels by force, because the mountains were a difficult stronghold to attack from outside and the rebels had many sympathizers in the Medan area. After three years of curious and patient negotiations, in 1961 peace was agreed to on condition that none of the rebels be punished. Boyke thus returned to Medan. The leaders of the rebellion were permitted to open private enterprises in Java. Boyke remained in Medan and was appointed vice-director of the East Sumatra Branch of the National Oil Corporation (Pertamina), but he failed to establish a good relationship with the director. One day, his miserable body was found dead after falling from the top of the radio tower near to Pertamina's official residence, in an apparent suicide. The cause of his death was actually rumored to be a homicide. His father, Dr. Nainggolan, proposed examining the body personally but was not permitted to by the government. Dr. Nainggolan being unconvinced, died soon after, in deep grief and discontent. How sad and pitiful was the fate of the Nainggolan family! The taxi driver that I had hired for three days, incidentally, had been a driver for Boyke when he was a commander. The driver still admired his brave commander and showed me his grave in Brastagi.

SEEING ISMED AGAIN

Because of my strong desire to find some of my former dear friends, I visited the house of Purungan in Padan Bulan Street where I had often enjoyed pleasant conversations with Batak youths. The family of Purungan had also moved to Java, but the person who lived there was fortunately a relative and gave me some useful information on Ismed, whom I was closest to. The cheerful fighter of the Fifth Corps had, unbeknownst to me, been working at the Indonesian Embassy in Tokyo for five years already.

As soon as I returned to Tokyo, I got in touch with Ismed, and resumed our old friendship after thirty years. He was an important man now whom I did not address without using an honorific title. When I met him, he asked me about my study of Batak folklore. Hearing that my records were still on my bookshelf as a handwritten manuscript, he eagerly advised me to publish them as a textbook for the Japanese to understand the Indonesian people, and he kindly recommended the manuscript to the Japan-Indonesian Association. It was consequently published and is now functioning as a useful textbook for Japanese businessmen going to Sumatra. Ismed also spoke kindly of my efforts in the Tebing Tinggi incident to the members of the embassy. The young blood of my youth immediately ran through my old body and my heart was filled with emotion. I will always love the Indonesians.

POSTSCRIPT

In 1979, I again visited Sumatra at the invitation of the Freedom Fighters Veteran Council in the Medan area, supported by the North Sumatra government. This was because my contribution to Indonesian independence had been revealed by a recent study of the history of the independence struggle in the Medan area. I thus spent one very emotional week recalling my youth when I made a strenuous effort, with burning passion, for Indonesia's national goals.

Many countries became independent as a result of the momentum built by the Pacific War. The age of colonialism is over and a perfect friendship has been established between the Netherlands and the Republic of Indonesia. Many Indonesian students are studying in the Netherlands. Many Dutch tourists are visiting Indonesia. The relationship is closer than with many other countries.

The world is now shifting from a nationalism based on individual countries to one based on expanded communities linked geographically, racially, financially, historically, and/or politically, with globalism as the final goal. Such an internationalism can only be stable when based on sound assembled nationalisms. I am now enjoying a happy, peaceful life as an old scientist who made some contribution to international human welfare. But, at the same time, I am also enjoying my past memories of a time when I burned with passion for nationalism.

www.ingramcontent.com/pod-product-compliance
Lightning Source LLC
Chambersburg PA
CBHW020653230426
43665CB00008B/420